Cambridge Elements

Elements in the Politics of Development
edited by
Rachel Beatty Riedl
Einaudi Center for International Studies and Cornell University
Ben Ross Schneider
Massachusetts Institute of Technology
Maya Tudor
Oxford University

Mario Einaudi
CENTER FOR
INTERNATIONAL STUDIES

THE UNDULATING CAPACITY OF THE STATE

Autochthony and Infrastructure Development in African Cities

Ato Kwamena Onoma
University of Toronto

Shaftesbury Road, Cambridge CB2 8EA, United Kingdom

One Liberty Plaza, 20th Floor, New York, NY 10006, USA

477 Williamstown Road, Port Melbourne, VIC 3207, Australia

314–321, 3rd Floor, Plot 3, Splendor Forum, Jasola District Centre, New Delhi – 110025, India

103 Penang Road, #05–06/07, Visioncrest Commercial, Singapore 238467

Cambridge University Press is part of Cambridge University Press & Assessment, a department of the University of Cambridge.

We share the University's mission to contribute to society through the pursuit of education, learning and research at the highest international levels of excellence.

www.cambridge.org
Information on this title: www.cambridge.org/9781009698375

DOI: 10.1017/9781009698382

© Ato Kwamena Onoma 2025

This publication is in copyright. Subject to statutory exception and to the provisions of relevant collective licensing agreements, no reproduction of any part may take place without the written permission of Cambridge University Press & Assessment.

When citing this work, please include a reference to the DOI 10.1017/9781009698382

First published 2025

A catalogue record for this publication is available from the British Library

ISBN 978-1-009-69837-5 Hardback
ISBN 978-1-009-69839-9 Paperback
ISSN 2515-1584 (online)
ISSN 2515-1576 (print)

Cambridge University Press & Assessment has no responsibility for the persistence or accuracy of URLs for external or third-party internet websites referred to in this publication and does not guarantee that any content on such websites is, or will remain, accurate or appropriate.

For EU product safety concerns, contact us at Calle de José Abascal, 56, 1°, 28003 Madrid, Spain, or email eugpsr@cambridge.org

The Undulating Capacity of the State

Autochthony and Infrastructure Development in African Cities

Elements in the Politics of Development

DOI: 10.1017/9781009698382
First published online: August 2025

Ato Kwamena Onoma
University of Toronto

Author for correspondence: Ato Kwamena Onoma, ato.onoma@utoronto.ca

Abstract: This Element weaves together literatures on autochthony and belonging and on African urbanism to shed new light on the ability of the African state to undertake development interventions in some of the most important urban centers on the continent. It explains variations in levels of trust in the African state that shape neighborhoods' responses to states' development interventions. Focusing on the Senegalese state's construction of the VDN 2 highway on the outskirts of the capital, Dakar, the author argues that in major African cities with colonial origins, whether neighborhoods project themselves as "autochthonous" or "migrant" communities shapes general attitudes toward the state and influences the capacity of the state to carry out development interventions in these areas. In these cities, states are more likely to successfully intervene in neighborhoods dominated by "new" migrants to the city than in those neighborhoods that portray themselves as "autochthones" of these cities.

Keywords: state capacity, autochthony, infrastructure development, Senegal, colonial cities

© Ato Kwamena Onoma 2025

ISBNs: 9781009698375 (HB), 9781009698399 (PB), 9781009698382 (OC)
ISSNs: 2515-1584 (online), 2515-1576 (print)

Contents

1 Introduction   1

2 On State Capacity in Africa   10

3 Autochthony and the Undulating Capacity of the State   18

4 Cambérène: Intervening among Guarded Autochthons   23

5 Parcelles Assainies: Highway Construction in a "New" Neighborhood   36

6 Conclusion   46

   List of Abbreviations   53

   References   54

1 Introduction

On a weekday evening in February 2020, Mbissine[1] made her way from work at the center of the Senegalese capital, Dakar, to a new residential estate northeast of the city. She drove smoothly along the VDN (Voie de Dégagement Nord) highway, past the coast of the neighborhood of Parcelles Assainies, until she reached the edge of the nearby commune of Cambérène. There, the highway abruptly metamorphosed into a roughly 1-km dirt track and detour through a densely populated neighborhood, along which her car crawled in heavy traffic for about an hour. She felt a deep sense of relief when she finally rejoined the free-flowing traffic on the VDN highway after crossing Cambérène. In this Element, I seek to make sense of why the Senegalese state was able to construct a segment of the VDN 2 highway along the coast of Parcelles Assainies with relative ease within a year while struggling for over four years to build an adjacent segment of the same highway along the coast of the adjoining neighborhood of Cambérène. I use this puzzle to address the broader question of why African states demonstrate significant capacity to undertake some development interventions but struggle at implementing others.

I argue that in Africa's colonial cities, the capacity of states to implement development interventions is higher in neighborhoods that self-identify as agglomerations of recent migrants than in those that claim autochthony in these cities. In Africa, the process of claiming autochthony in cities with colonial origins (Rayfield 1974; Southall 1989; Coquery-Vidrovitch 1991; Bocquier 2004; Freund 2007) has pitted communities that cast themselves as autochthonous in fierce struggles against colonial and postcolonial states that infringe on their land rights (Goerg 2006; Onoma 2013; Osseo-Asare 2016; Njoh 2017). These ongoing struggles over land rights have created a heightened distrust of the state. This has enhanced the inclination of these neighborhoods to challenge the state, making it difficult for states to implement development interventions in their midst. The residents of Cambérène cast their neighborhood as an autochthonous one and their fierce contestation of the state's effort to build the VDN 2 caused the state to struggle over four years and over run its budget to build that segment of the highway.

There is greater trust in the state and its interventions in neighborhoods dominated by more recent migrants, who often relate to the state as a provider and guarantor, even if a rather inconstant and unreliable one, of land rights and public goods. While autochthonous neighborhoods tend to center the creation and presence of the state as a problem, it is the absence of the state that neighborhoods dominated by new migrants view as problematic. While

---

[1] This is a fictive name to ensure the anonymity of this study participant.

autochthonous neighborhoods often focus on what (land) the state has taken from them, neighborhoods dominated by migrants tend to focus on land and public goods that the state has or has not (yet) offered them. These migrant neighborhoods are more trusting of the state and its interventions, often decrying only the insufficient level of such interventions. These neighborhoods offer lesser resistance to state projects, making it easier for states to carry out development interventions in these communities. Parcelles Assainies' residents celebrate their neighborhood as a hub of migrants to the city, and this eased the state's construction of the VDN 2 highway on their coast.

I conceive of state capacity here in the sense of Mann's (1984, 189) "infrastructural power," which he defined as "the capacity of the state to actually penetrate civil society, and to implement logistically political decisions throughout the realm." I follow in the steps of scholars (Hyden 1980; Scott 1999; 2009) that approach this capacity as inherently relational and partly dependent on how society perceives the state. I center large-scale infrastructure projects as fields for the accumulation, performance, exercise and contestation of this power (Mcfarlane and Rutherford 2008; Njoh 2009; Weinstein 2013; Ranganathan 2014; Harvey and Knox 2015; Appel, Anand, and Gupta 2018; Di Nunzio 2018). The central argument of this Element is shown in Figure 1.

The VDN, the project that is the focus of this manuscript, is a major highway that runs from Place OMVS/Bourguiba in the Senegalese capital to the village of Tivaouane Peulh on the northern outskirts of the city. The 32 km highway was constructed in three phases between 2007 and 2022. The VDN 1 was constructed in 2007–2008 with funding from the Islamic Development Bank and the Government of Senegal. It is 6 km long and runs from Place OMVS/Bourguiba to CICES in Dakar. Because of funding issues, the Senegalese state followed this up with the VDN 3, which is 17.3 km long and runs from Golf Guédiawaye on the outskirts of Dakar to the village of Tivaouane Peulh in 2013–2016. The VDN 3 was also constructed with funds from the Kuwait Fund and the Government of Senegal. In 2017, the state commenced the construction of the VDN 2 to connect the already operational VDN 1 and VDN 3. The VDN 2 is 8.7 km long and runs from CICES to Golf Guédiawaye. A fourth phase of the VDN is supposed to take the highway from the village of Tivaouane Peulh to the city of Diamniadio, where it will connect with another major highway, the Autoroute à Péage.

The VDN is part of an outburst of large-scale infrastructural development in Senegal that started under President Abdoulaye Wade, who ruled the country from 2000 to 2012. This process continued at a feverish pace under Macky Sall, who governed the country from 2012 to 2024. During his rule, Abdoulaye Wade remade the profile of Dakar with major road projects like the Corniche Ouest,

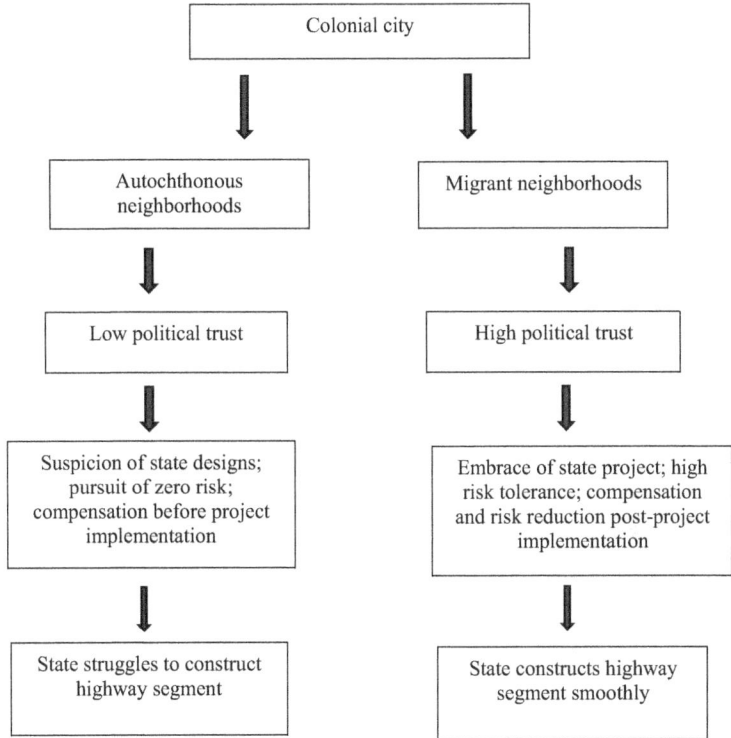

Figure 1 The argument with causal mechanisms.

the VDN 1, and the Autoroute, which became a toll road – Autoroute à Péage – as it snaked out of the capital. He also built the Musée des Civilisations Noires, the Grand Théâtre National, and the Monument de la Renaissance Africaine. Away from the city, Abdoulaye Wade built a new international airport (Aéroport International Blaise Diagne) at Diass and commenced work on the construction of a new city at Diamniadio.

On assuming power in 2012, Macky Sall maintained the focus on large-scale infrastructure development. He completed the second and third phases of the VDN project and continued work on the Autoroute à Péage, extending it to Mbour and connecting it to newly constructed highways to the cities of Thiès and Touba. He finished work on the airport at Diass, continued work on the new city of Diamniadio, and commenced work on the construction of a deep seaport at Bargny. He built the Train Express Régional (TER) between Dakar and Diamniadio and a Bus Rapid Transit (BRT) system in Dakar. He also embellished Dakar with the construction of multiple flyovers in his Projet de construction de 18 ponts et autoponts.

The bout of infrastructural development in Senegal is part of a growing trend of heavy investment in large-scale infrastructures, including highways, rail systems, seaports, dams, sports infrastructure, housing estates, and whole new cities across Africa and the rest of the Global South since the turn of the twenty-first century (Boeck 2011; Alves 2013; Ren and Weinstein 2013; Nugent 2018; Adunbi 2019; Jedwab and Storeygard 2019; Splinter and Van Leynseele 2019; Chiyemura, Gambino, and Zajontz 2023). The African Union's Program for Infrastructure Development in Africa (PIDA) is actively promoting this investment in infrastructure on the continent as an important element of the organization's Agenda 2063.[2]

A July 2017 YouTube video released by the Senegalese state's Agence des Travaux et de Gestion des Routes au Sénégal (AGEROUTE Sn), the state structure responsible for the construction, maintenance, and repair of roads, placed the VDN project at the heart of the state's effort to boost growth, reduce poverty, and improve the quality of life of its citizenry through its Plan Sénégal Émergent.[3] As has been done by builders of similar transportation infrastructure projects around the world (Harvey and Knox 2015), the Senegalese state cited the need to ease the movement of goods and people to promote local and national economies to justify this investment.

As Nugent (2018) has pointed out, this spate of infrastructure development raises important questions about the capacity and developmental ambition of African states. These large-scale infrastructure projects suggest that African states are not as bereft of developmental ambition and capacity as was suggested by a vibrant Afropessimist literature (Joseph 2003; Ayittey 1993; van Arkadie 1995; Bayart 1993; Chabal and Daloz 1999; Bayart, Ellis, and Hibou 1999). The future orientation of many of these projects also suggests a recapturing of the spirit of planning that marked the immediate post-independence epoch, which was subsequently banished in favor of structural adjustment in the 1980s and 1990s (Mkandawire 2001; Diagne 2004). But some have pointed to failures of prioritization and corruption in these projects that have plunged many countries into debt traps involving new funders like China, Turkey, and Gulf countries (Hollands 2007; Asongu and Aminkeng 2013; Alves 2013; Singh 2020). Also, these projects often lack the linear trajectory invoked in the narratives of leaders with many such schemes "suspended, abandoned, delayed or deferred" (Appel, Anand, and Gupta 2018, 18; also see Holland 2023). In this Element, I use the

---

[2] See "Program Infrastructure Development for Africa (PIDA)" on the African Union Commission website. https://au.int/en/ie/pida. Also see the page on partnerships on the African Development Bank website. www.afdb.org/en/topics-and-sectors/initiatives-partnerships.

[3] See "Prolongement de la VDN2: Tronçon CICES – Golf club Guédiawaye" by Ageroute Sn. www.youtube.com/watch?v=V3B4__i4Rag.

Senegalese state's work on the VDN as a prism to examine the varying levels of capacity of African states to undertake large-scale infrastructure projects.

1.1 An Uneven Process of Implementation

The variation I explain in this manuscript is the relative ease with which the Senegalese state was able to undertake work on the VDN 2 project along the coasts of two neighboring municipalities in Dakar. While the Senegalese state was eventually able to construct the highway along the coasts of both municipalities, it did so with much more difficulty in Cambérène than in Parcelles Assainies.

The VDN 2 was supposed to run through the neighborhoods of HLM Grande Médine and Diamalaye II and along the coast of Parcelles Assainies and Cambérène. Under the supervision of Ageroute SN, a partnership of the Moroccan firms SINTRAM and HOUAR started work on the highway in 2017. SINTRAM-HOUAR quickly completed work along the Parcelles Assainies coast, and this segment of the road was opened to traffic in 2018. Despite starting work on the Cambérène segment at the same time, the state struggled for over four years before finally completing that section of the highway in March 2022 due to contestation by community members.

Fierce contestation of the road-building project by the community in Cambérène frequently interrupted construction on the site, forced the builders to demolish already completed work, and even abandon the site altogether in early 2019. The lengthy construction process, constant changes, and the undoing and redoing of sections caused the government to run out of project funds, forcing it to seek additional funds to enable the completion of the project. With the rest of the highway completed and functional, the uncompleted segment at Cambérène became notorious for intense traffic jams for almost three years.[4] It was only in March 2022, three years after the completion of the rest of the highway, that the state completed and opened that section of the road (Leral.net 2022).

1.2 Study Design, Case Selection, and Methods

In this Element, I hold the state, its planned intervention, and the broad geographical zone of intervention constant to examine the effect of neighborhood types on the capacity of the state to undertake development interventions. I exploit many of the benefits of subnational comparison (Snyder 2001; Enriquez, Sybblis, and

---

[4] A video clip of coverage of the highway in the 8pm news of the national TV station RTS1 on September 20, 2019, posted to YouTube by the Ministère des Infrastructures, des Transports Terrestres et du Désenclavement shows the completed sections of the highway as well as the gaping chasm around the neighborhood of Cambérène that separates the two completed segments of the highway. www.youtube.com/watch?v=8BOHonznR00.

Centeno 2017; Sellers 2019) in analyzing the VDN 2 construction exercise along the coast of the two proximate neighborhoods of Dakar. The choice of cases gives me variation in the key outcome across space. The state struggled to construct the highway in Cambérène but did so with relative ease in Parcelles Assainies. This divergence is puzzling because it flouts the predictions of some theories that are influential in the study of contemporary African political economy. The sameness of the state's planned intervention renders unhelpful theories that focus on types of tasks in making sense of variations in state capacity. The idea that states can be better at undertaking some tasks than others is at the heart of Mann's (1984) distinction between the autonomous and infrastructural power of the state and has influenced a large literature on the developmental state (Evans 1995; Kohli 2004). Here, we observe a marked difference in the capacity of the state to implement the same project, suggesting a need to look beyond types of state capacity in making sense of this divergence in outcomes.

The proximity and similarity of the terrain along which construction work took place across the two neighborhoods suggest that literatures emphasizing geography and spatiality in making sense of states' ability to dominate and shape their territories (Johnston 1991; Diamond 1999; Herbst 2000; Scott 2009) may be of limited utility here. Road construction in both neighborhoods was supposed to take place in a sandy and flat coastal terrain where the activities of fishermen are limited compared to neighborhoods like Yoff and Soumbedioune in the city. Further, both areas are municipalities in Dakar, the capital city of Senegal, where the presence and capacity of the Senegalese state is probably at its maximum across the national territory. This eliminates the challenges that may come with comparing areas of a country where the presence and power of the state varies. This variation is often highlighted by literature that sees African states' presence as largely concentrated in capital cities and less present in peripheral areas far from these capital cities (Herbst 2000). In this work I draw inspiration from Boone's (2003) more nuanced account of variation in the geographical spread of state capacity and presence in Africa that goes beyond the question of distance from the capital city. I also draw on the resolute focus of Hoelscher et al. (2023, 4) on disparate "geographies of citizenship practice" across the same urban terrains that can shed light on political economic outcomes in contemporary Africa.

The choice of these two cases also affords variation in the self-projected identities of these communities, which, I argue, influences their level of trust in and inclination to oppose the state and its projects. The idea that their neighborhood is an autochthonous one is central to how people in Cambérène portray their community. This differs from identity discourses among residents of Parcelles Assainies, which often dwell on the recent settlement of people of diverse origins.

This divergence, I argue, has significant implications for how these communities see and interact with the state and explains the difference in how construction work on the VDN 2 fared along the coast of Cambérène and Parcelles Assainies.

This ability to focus on the origins and workings of different levels of political trust is facilitated by my choice of two cases that are both renowned for their capacity to confront the state. While autochthonous neighborhoods like Cambérène are often cast as particularly capable of collective action, Parcelles Assainies has distinguished itself over the years as a veritable cauldron of youth activism and the bane of abusive state leaders in Senegal. This capacity of people in Parcelles Assainies to engage in collective action to confront the state will come as no surprise to scholars of urban politics. The high and dense population of the neighborhood, along with the multitude of service delivery challenges that residents face, is noted in the literature as likely to boost communities' capacity for collective action and activism against the state (Bates 1981; 1993; Hoelscher et al. 2023).

The unit of analysis in this work is the formal administrative unit referred to as the "commune d'arrondissement." Parcelles Assainies and Cambérène are two of the nineteen communes d'arrondissement in the Department of Dakar, which constitutes the capital city of Senegal. The communes of the Department of Dakar are shown in Figure 2. The Department of Dakar is, in turn, one of five departments in the wider Region of Dakar, which is one of the fourteen regions that make up Senegal.

My use of both "municipalities" and "neighborhoods" to characterize these units mirrors common usage in Dakar. While the official designations and boundaries are important, these communes have subdivisions that are also agglomerations of other smaller units, and so on. Like questions of identity, the level of agglomeration that people emphasize in speech and action is highly contextual and political. The struggles over the VDN 2 often involved people who frequently made claims in the name of these agglomerations at the commune level.

I employ a mix of archival research, ethnography, the exploration of media coverage, and semi-structured interviews to make sense of the politics surrounding road construction in these two communes. While each of these methods contributed unique elements to this inquiry, their juxtaposition enabled me to triangulate sources in a murky environment of competing narratives.

This work benefited greatly from the immersion that ethnography permits (Schatz 2009; Wedeen 2010). Between 2017 and 2022, I resided in the neighborhood of Golf Sud, which shares borders with Cambérène and I used the VDN 1 and VDN 2 as the main routes for my daily commute. Between 2017 and the start of the COVID-19 pandemic in Senegal in early 2020, I spent a lot of time in Cambérène and Parcelles Assainies observing construction work on the

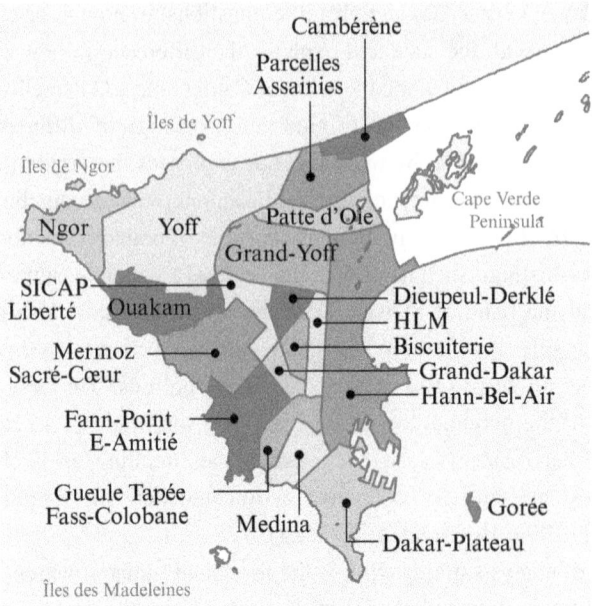

Figure 2 Dakar and its communes.
Source: Mikima, CC BY-SA 3.0 https://creativecommons.org/licenses/by-sa/3.0, via Wikimedia Commons

highway, demonstrations by community members, efforts by the police and gendarmerie to curb these demonstrations and the multiple visits by high-level state officials to showcase the project and seek common ground with communities. I held long and repeated informal discussions with many residents of Parcelles Assainies, Cambérène, and Guédiawaye as part of this immersion.

I complemented my observation of the political dynamics in which the VDN 2 construction was enmeshed with semi-structured in-depth interviews with forty-seven people in Dakar from July 2018 to October 2019. These interviewees included community activists, local leaders, and ordinary citizens in Cambérène, Parcelles Assainies, and the nearby neighborhoods of Diamalaye II and Golf Guédiawaye. I was also able to conduct an extended interview with a senior official of AGEROUTE Sn. The relatively free rein that interviewees enjoy during semi-structured interviews (Fujii 2017) allowed the sharing of thoughts that alerted me to some of the dynamics that I explore here.

Media has been a source of significant information for this project. Like many major infrastructure projects that assume great political relevance (Willems 2019), the VDN project occupied an important place in Senegal's democratic politics and received significant media attention. The state produced slick media content selling the project in the run-up to the 2019 presidential elections, and media houses sympathetic to the government took great interest in covering the progress of the project. More critical media houses went to great lengths to cover the problems that beset the project. Community groups also extensively used the media to air their grievances and share their version of events surrounding the project. Ethnographic immersion and semi-structured interviews helped me make sense of this treasure trove of information. As scholars of qualitative methods (Scott 1990; Alina-Pisano 2009; Fujii 2010; Sandberg 2010) have counseled, the goal of this exercise went beyond the determination of the truth or falsity of claims. I was particularly interested in what narratives revealed about narrators and the structures of power in which they were enmeshed.

This work falls within the comparative historical tradition (Thelen 2004; Thelen and Mahoney 2015). To borrow the words of Thelen and Mahoney (2015, 12), it grapples with the macro-structural dynamics of state-society relations by exploring "observed outcomes ... in particular times and places, and it does so by developing explanations that identify the causal mechanisms that enable and generate these outcomes." It centers temporality, a major preoccupation of the comparative historical tradition (Mahoney 2004; Thelen and Mahoney 2015). First, in fashioning an explanation, I examine processes over a long duration of time going back to the early days of the Dakar's foundation in the mid 1800s that have shaped highway construction in these neighborhoods in the early twenty-first century. Second, I pay significant attention to when, instead of just whether, events and processes unfolded (Thelen and Mahoney 2015, 20). In this vein I focus on the date of arrival of various groups in Dakar, instead of whether groups live in the city. I similarly focus on when, relative to the completion of work on the highway, aggressive resistance of the state's interventions occurred instead of just whether it took place. Finally, I consider the duration over which processes take place. It is in this light that I focus on how long it took the state to construct segments of the highway in neighboring municipalities instead of whether it was eventually able to do so.

Multiple rounds of archival research between July 2019 and May 2022 in the Senegalese National Archives (Archives nationales du Sénégal) in Dakar contributed significantly to my ability to privilege temporality in this work. I examined official documents relating to the early days of the French colony in the Cap Vert Peninsula, where Dakar is located, the spread of colonial authority in the area, and contestation over the gradual takeover of lands from Lébou communities. I was also able to access rare secondary materials concerning the early history of the Cap Vert Peninsula, where Dakar is located.

The rest of this Element is divided into five sections. Section 2 lays the ground for the principal argument of this work by reviewing significant developments in the literature on state capacity in Africa. I highlight major advances as well as challenges that are often rooted in a failure to take full account of the heterogeneity of state capacity across space and time on the continent. In Section 3, I contribute to the literature parsed in Section 2 by arguing that linking autochthony and identity politics on the continent with reflections on colonial cities in Africa can help us explain variations in the capacity of African states to carry out major development interventions across neighborhoods in colonial cities on the continent. Section 4 examines the state's difficulties with constructing a segment of the VDN 2 highway along the coast of Cambérène. In Section 5, I explore the far smoother effort of the state to construct the same highway along the coast of the commune of Parcelles Assainies. I summarize the central argument of the Element, situate it in broader political economy debates, and distill some of its policy implications in Section 6.

2 On State Capacity in Africa

When people revolt, the constructors are forced to stop the work. We talk to the people to find a solution to the problem and then go back to constructors to see how the design can be changed. The constructors tell us the additional cost and time needed to effect the changes. Sometimes construction is suspended because we have to go and seek additional funds to deal with all of this.
(A senior official of Ageroute SN commenting on the dynamics of construction work on the VDN 2 in an interview on October 2, 2019)

The swashbuckling, infrastructure-building African state of the early twenty-first century seems to differ considerably from the image of the "lame leviathan" painted by Callaghy (1987). This image of the African state as severely lacking in capacity was particularly rife from the 1980s to the turn of the century (Jackson 1990; Mazrui 1995; Grindle 1996; Herbst 2000; Mbembe 2001; Joseph 2003). Scholars pointed at many ways in which this weakness was said to manifest itself. They indicated that African states lacked the ability to build cohesive nation-states and maintain a significant presence across their territories (Jackson 1990; Reno 1998; Herbst 2000; Joseph 2003). They pointed out that this absence of the state was partly evident in its weak provision of public goods (Gough and Wood 2004; Seay 2010), allowing NGOs to assume many functions that are often thought of as states' responsibilities (Cammett and MacLean 2014; Benton 2015; Kushner and MacLean 2015). Scholars cast the low capacity of African states as similarly evident in the inability to carry out development work including policy making, implementation, and coordination, the creation and reinforcement of institutions that support economic activities, and the fostering of economic actors. They portrayed African states as lacking the legal rational bureaucratic forms of the developmental states of Asia (Evans 1995; van Arkadie 1995; Callaghy and Ravenhill 1993; Lewis and Stein 1997; Haggard 2018; Young 2018) with institutions taking more personalistic and patrimonial forms (Ayittey 1993; Bayart, Ellis, and Hibou 1999; Chabal and Daloz 1999; Mbembe 2001).

One can identify two distinct but related orientations in the literature that have dwelt on the weakness of African states. A patently neoliberal perspective regards the state as legitimate only insofar as it acts strictly as a handmaid of the market. Interventions by the state beyond this limited sphere are regarded as inappropriate and counterproductive and are said to be responsible for the economic crises that afflicted many African states that had taken the dirigiste path immediately after independence (World Bank 1981; Sender and Smith 1985; Landell-Mills, Agarwala, and Please 1989). Forcefully promoted on the continent by the Bretton Woods Institutions, especially during the era of structural adjustment programs of the 1980s and 1990s, this school of thought cast the problem of the African state as its bloated and over-extended character that made it impossible for it to effectively play this limited role (World Bank 1997; Olukoshi 1998; Mkandawire and Soludo 1999; Mkandawire 2001). The African state in this narrative was a bumbling actor whose form undermined its efforts to achieve its developmental goals.

A second perspective on the weakness of states' capacity in Africa has gone beyond the inability of African states to perform the core functions associated with states to focus on their disordering effects. The African state, in this literature, is often cast as an anti-developmental (instead of non-developmental) entity whose negative activities include the deliberate promotion of disorder, instability, and criminality. Instead of bumbling institutions, key state actors and institutions in this literature are cast as deliberately cultivating and exploiting disorder in the pursuit of personal economic and political ends (Bayart 1993; Bayart, Ellis, and Hibou 1999; Chabal and Daloz 1999; Mbembe 2001).

The narrative on African state incapacity has led in two distinct directions at the level of praxis. One focuses on making the state better. That is the discourse on reform that institutions like the World Bank and the IMF forcefully promoted on the continent as part of their neoliberal reform programs. The reforms carried out under neoliberal programs have often been portrayed as a process of "shrinking" (Feigenbaum, Henig, and Hamnett 1998) or "rolling back" (Beckman 1991; Mkandawire 2001) the state. The drastic reduction of the state was evident in the massive retrenchment of state workers, the privatization of parastatals, radical budget cuts, deregulation, and decentralization processes

(Beckman 1991; Naim 1994; Mkandawire and Soludo 1999; Ndegwa and Levy 2003; Idrissa Abdoulaye 2021). Belying the narrative of "shrinking," these reforms have also included the creation and reinforcement of "market-enhancing institutions" like title registries, central banks, and judiciaries (Naim 1994; World Bank 2002; Onoma 2009), in line with Polanyi's (2001) portrayal of capitalism as involving a mass of interventions to facilitate the market. Mkandawire (2001) has highlighted the fundamental clash between the ontological and ethical foundations of this narrative of reform. The literature which casts African states as *inherently* corrupt and patrimonial then counsels these very states to undertaken reforms that render them more legal-rational!

A second approach that is more consistent with the ontological foundations of this literature opts to dodge the state altogether and resort to the private sector, non-state actors, including NGOs and civil society organizations, to undertake development work (Gary 1996). Critics have noted that, while these entities may be capable of small-scale and temporary projects, their capacity to carry out interventions that effect largescale and sustained economic change is very limited (Nega and Schneider 2014). This is in addition to the fact that the vaunted independence of these entities from the state is questionable, with state officials sometimes leading, owning, and otherwise influencing so-called NGOs and civil society organizations (Osaghae 1997; Obadare 2005; Adebanwi 2017). Since the pervasive influence of the state makes efforts to bypass it in development work futile, it is paramount that we invest in understanding the state and its role in development in Africa better. It is this task that I contribute to in this Element.

2.1 Homogenization and the Promise of a Relational Approach

A significant challenge in this effort to make sense of states' influence on development outcomes in Africa lies in the tendency to homogenize the form and capacity of African states. The literature faces the problem of using a constant variable – the weak capacity of African states – to explain political-economic phenomena that vary across both time and space. Close attention to political dynamics on the African continent reveals that key political-economic outcomes, including levels of economic growth (Samatar 1999; Mkandawire 2001), public goods provision (Bates 1981; Mkandawire 2001), social policy implementation (Adesina 2021), and national integration (Boone 2003; Mann 2005; Mann 2008) vary significantly across space and time. As I point out in my earlier work (Onoma 2009), it is difficult for what is often cast as the uniformly weak capacity of these states to shed significant light on these varying outcomes.

The use of boundary conditions to excise countries and regions of the continent that would otherwise constitute anomalies in the narrative of state weakness is often tantamount to defining African states as a priori lacking in capacity. The first casualty of such excision has often been North Africa, reinforcing the long-existing but problematic tendency to separate that part of Africa from what is termed "Sub-Saharan Africa" (Herbst 2000; van de Walle 2001, 1). South Africa, and other countries like Botswana, Mauritius, Cape Verde, which have not always fitted the idea of a failed state, are also often removed from such analyses of "African states" (Herbst 2000; Van de Walle 2001, 3). The temporal aspect of political economic success and failure problematizes things even further. Many of the states that were regarded as economic catastrophes during the era of structural adjustment had demonstrated impressive growth rates that even surpassed some of the best performers in Africa under neoliberal economic reforms (Mkandawire 2001). Others like Ghana, Uganda, and Rwanda came back from periods of near collapse to demonstrate significant levels of growth and efficacious policy formulation and implementation (Rothchild 1991; Dijkstra and Van Donge 2001; Purdeková 2011).

A more rewarding approach that I adopt in this work is to embrace and exploit diversity in the continent's political economies to advance the task of explanation. The literature on pockets of effectiveness has taken halting steps in this direction, arguing that even a weak state can sometimes have islands of productivity because the agglomeration of bureaucracies that make up the state often operates in silos, between which competencies do not easily percolate (Daland 1981; Schneider 1991; Strauss 1998; Grindle 2004; Owusu 2006; Leonard 2008; Prichard and Leonard 2010). While this silo structure insulates peculiarly effective bureaucracies from contamination by the morass that plagues other segments of the state, it also ensures that the high-performing character of certain agencies does not infiltrate into other areas of the state (Prichard and Leonard 2010). Efforts at building and reinforcing islands of effectiveness during neoliberal economic reforms in Africa targeted central banks and ministries of finance (Olukoshi 1998; Mkandawire 1999; 2001). Benton (2015) describes similar efforts at transforming HIV/AIDS commissions and secretariats into pockets of effectiveness during the height of the global fight against the disease. Explanations of these islands of effectiveness have focused on reforms (Grindle and Thomas 1991; Heredia and Schneider 2003), leadership and management (Grindle 1997; Leonard 2008), institutional functions (Moore and Schneider 2004; Leonard 2008), and the location of institutions in the broader state apparatus and political economy (Grindle and Thomas 1991; Heredia and Schneider 2003; Kaufman 2003; Moore and Schneider 2004).

While a valuable corrective to the dominant narrative on state weakness in Africa, the literature on pockets of effectiveness is fundamentally informed by the same logic of pervasive state incapacity in Africa that one sees in much of the literature. Because of this, it is best suited to and explicitly set up to explain *unexpected and puzzling* islands of capacity in a sea of ineffectiveness. This a priori framing of evidence of capacity and effectiveness as puzzling means that it is likely to under-diagnose cases of strong capacity and ultimately lacks the ability to explain variation beyond exceptional "islands."

Mann's (1984; 2008) reflections on what he terms state power is another promising approach to state capacity that has, unfortunately, been subsumed by the homogenizing literature on weak state capacity in Africa. Mann distinguishes between the despotic power of the state – "range of actions which the elite is empowered to undertake without routine, institutionalized negotiation with civil society" (1984, 188) – and its infrastructural power – "the capacity of the state to actually penetrate civil society, and to implement logistically political decisions throughout the realm" (1984, 189) or more simply, to engage in "binding rulemaking" (1984, 190). Unfortunately, scholars have tended to wield Mann's (1984) distinction within the same homogenizing logic that plagues work on African states. Scholars have often just switched from generalizing statements about the weakness of African states to more nuanced statements about the lack of infrastructural capacity of African states, often comparing these states with those elsewhere in Asia and Latin America that demonstrate more capacity (Evans 1995; Kohli 2004; Haggard 2018).

Mann's insistence on "civil society" (1984, 188–189) in his definition of state power suggests a relational approach that provides a pathway out of the quagmire of homogenization, which undermines much work on African states. It facilitates the embrace and exploitation of heterogeneity in analyses of state capacity on the continent. A relational approach to state capacity stresses the fact that many state interventions involve interactions with societies that are imbued with preferences, interests, and outlooks of their own. Understanding the ability of the state to achieve its developmental goals – engage in "binding rulemaking" (Mann 1984, 190) – thus requires a focus that goes beyond the state to also look at the social actors that it interacts with. Going beyond the zero-sum view of this relationship (Hyden 1980; Migdal 1988; Hyden 2008), scholars have shown that while societal opposition to state plans can make their achievement difficult, social acceptance and embrace of state projects can enhance states' ability to implement their policies (Amsden 1989; Evans 1995; Schneider 1998; Doner and Schneider 2000). This expansive understanding of state–society interactions raises the central question I tackle in this Element. Why do some segments of society embrace state projects, boosting the ability of the state to attain its objectives, while others oppose such interventions, undermining the capacity of the state to achieve its goals.

2.2 Who Wants a Highway?

There is a laudatory narrative on roads that leads one to expect massive social support for their construction. Scholars point out that the development of transportation systems, including major highways, contributes to economic growth and social wellbeing (Njoh 2000; Limao and Venables 2001; Ndulu 2006) by facilitating the movement of goods and people, boosting tourism (Njoh 2000; Sietchiping, Permezel, and Ngomsi 2012; Agbiboa 2020) and enabling the provision of services (Ndulu 2006; Calderon and Servén 2014). Transportation networks, scholars argue, also promote the spread of states across their territories (Migdal 1988; Herbst 2000; Currie, Otero-Bahamon, and Uribe 2021; Müller-Crepon, Hunziker and Cederman 2021) as well as regional integration (Akpan 2014; Geda and Seid 2015).

These celebratory discourses on transportation infrastructure gloss over the contentious roles these networks and the process of constructing them have all too often played in socio-political life, which has earned them suspicion in certain segments of society. The development of road networks is part of what Scott calls "distance-demolishing" (Scott 2009, 11) or "space-conquering" technologies (Scott 2009, 20) that have further integrated marginal communities into oppressive and exploitative political-economic arrangements (Scott 2009, 166; Ferrante, Andrade, and Fearnside 2021). Gentrification, for instance, has sometimes been facilitated by infrastructure (re)development in major cities across the globe (Harvey 2003; Levenson 2018; Di Nunzio 2022). Further, political authorities have sometimes used major highways to further isolate marginal communities, carve them up in ways that hinder the ability of their residents to engage in collective action, and demolish their most vital zones (Fotsch 2007; Mohl 2014; McClintock 2015; Archer 2020). These concerns have understandably fueled agitation over the construction of major transportation infrastructure.

Here, I exploit the possibilities offered by literatures that are sometimes presented as two opposing ways of understanding local agitation over infrastructure projects. While one view presents such agitation as part of a logic of rejection, the other casts it as informed by a logic of extraction. I argue here that the common thread of state–society relations that binds these two approaches offers a pathway toward a nuanced understanding of state capacity to engage in development work in Africa.

The literature on the NIMBY (not-in-my-backyard) phenomenon is emblematic of the view of such activism as being informed by a logic of rejection. Projects targeted by NIMBY agitation often supply public goods that many in wider society would readily recognize as important for society. Despite this, locals' objections to their location in their neighborhoods, due to concerns over pollution, local living conditions, and property values, provoke an undersupply of these goods (Dear 1992; Wolsink 2000; Schively 2007, 256; Wang et al. 2021; Foster and Warren 2022). States and other opponents of NIMBYism have often castigated it as narrow self-interested and even irrational activism that undermines the public good (Gibson 2005, 381; Schively 2007, 257). More supportive voices point out that it sometimes takes the form of principled grassroots democratic organizing that has occasionally led to the improvement of these projects (Dear 1992, 288; Wolsink 2000, 59; Gibson 2005, 387; Schively 2007, 257–258; Weinstein and Ren 2009; Einstein, Glick, and Palmers 2020).

Holland (2023) offers another way of understanding local activism on infrastructure projects that casts it as informed by a logic of extraction. Locals, in this perspective, are very much interested in these projects or, at least, do not object to their development or location. Their goal is to extract as much compensation from the state as possible in exchange for allowing the projects' development (2023, 640). While Holland is careful to distinguish her outlook from analyses informed by the logic of rejection (2023, 640), the areas of convergence between these two approaches provide highly promising pathways for advancing our understanding of states' capacity to implement infrastructure projects.

One area of convergence concerns the nature of activism and the related questions of scale and level of measurement. Because there is usually a greater-than-zero chance of convincing most individuals and communities to accept an intervention with the right compensation and inducements, the question of whether projects are wanted or not by the local community may best be cast as a question of degree, to be measured as a continuous variable instead of a dichotomy, to be measured as a categorical and binary variable. There is also significant convergence in the solutions that are deployed by project implementers in response to such agitation. Incentives like "cash, jobs, local public goods, *and* infrastructure," mentioned by Holland (2023, 640), all feature in the list of concessions and inducements deployed to overcome and dull NIMBY activism (Dear 1992, 295; Schively 2007, 260; Holm et al. 2021, 8; Foster and Warren 2022, 149).

Further, both the logic of rejection and that of extraction go beyond the specific project under consideration to contemplate the extent to which communities have come to trust or distrust the state and its agents with whom they are interacting. Drawing on the work of Easton (1975, 447), Gouws and Schulz-Herzenberg (2016, 8) define trust as a sentiment that "is present when citizens feel that their own interests would be attended to even if the authorities were exposed to little supervision or scrutiny". Scholars recognize that this vertical form of trust – political trust – influences a wide range of outcomes that are at the heart of state capacity. These include policy implementation (Hutchison and Johnson 2011), tax compliance (Faizal et al. 2017), epidemic control and prevention (Obadare 2005), partisanship and support for leaders (Hetherington 1998), the broader effectiveness of the state (Putnam 1994; Putnam 1995) levels of development (Bratton and Gyimah-Boadi 2016), and democratic stability (Citrin and Stoker 2018).

The literature suggests four ways in which political trust can affect how local communities react to states' efforts to implement large-scale infrastructure projects. First, varying levels of political trust influence the extent to which communities buy into broad state narratives about these projects and the motivations behind their construction (Dear 1992, 292; Gibson 2005, 382). While trusting locals accept these narratives, locals who have little trust in the state often harbor suspicions about hidden malevolent motives behind these projects. Second, low levels of political trust also lead locals, unlike their more trusting compatriots, to suspect the state of deploying a bait-and-switch strategy – seeking their approval of plans that would then be substituted with alternatives that appear more sinister later. The refusal to buy into broad state narratives about projects and suspicions of a bait-and-switch strategy by the state, which are absent in communities with high levels of trust, can fuel local contestation of projects, delaying and sometimes even aborting them altogether.

Third, levels of political trust affect locals' calculation of risks (Schively 2007; Wang et al. 2021). Communities facing a state that they trust are likely to be more risk tolerant, believing that the state will be willing to bear the costs of dealing with negative externalities if they materialize in the future. Less trusting communities are likely to be highly risk averse because they believe that the state will not be there to offer relief in case of future disasters. Since reducing risks is a function of funds and time (Schively 2007), distrusting communities' relentless push for zero-risk project design and implementation can bloat the cost and duration of projects.

Fourth, levels of political trust can influence the temporal horizons of locals regarding risk reduction and inducements (Dear 1992, 295; Schively 2007, 260; Holm et al. 2021, 8; Foster and Warren 2022, 149; Holland 2023, 640). Communities that trust the state might allow it to work on reducing risks and providing compensation alongside or after the construction of the infrastructure project, easing project implementation. Those who see the state as untrustworthy will insist on the delivery of these benefits before the commencement of the infrastructure project, believing that once it completes work on the project, the state is likely to disappear without fulfilling its promises. Given the magnitude of risk reduction measures and inducement packages – parks, electricity, pipe-borne water, hospitals, sanitation systems, and schools (Foster and Warren 2022; Holland 2023) – requiring their complete delivery before the commencement of work on projects can delay project implementation for years.

Examining levels of political trust will, thus, help us make sense of the state's ability to implement large-scale infrastructure projects. Efforts by the same state to implement the same project will be marked by greater success in more trusting communities than in less trusting ones. Why, then, do some communities have greater trust in the state than others? In Section 3, I explain variations in the extent of trust in the state across urban neighborhoods in Africa's colonial cities. Then, in line with the extensive literature that notes the impact of trust on policy implementation and state and local government effectiveness (Obadare 2005; Faizal et al. 2017; Hutchison and Johnson 2017; Bob-Milliar and Lauterbach 2021; Resnick and Sivasubramanian 2023), I link this to the uneven trajectory of the Senegalese state's VDN 2 project.

3 Autochthony and the Undulating Capacity of the State

Why should we believe all that they are telling us about this road?
Community activist, Cambérène (July 10, 2018)

Mame Wally,[5] a retired civil servant and long-time resident of Parcelles Assainies in Dakar, can best be described as a firm believer in and advocate of state interventions to improve urban neighborhoods. During our many discussions, while I conducted research for this work, he demonstrated a high level of trust in the Senegalese state, often through flowery commentary on those that he cast as less trusting of the state. Mame Wally's topic of predilection was what he often referred to as "*les bizarreries*" (the oddities) of residents of the nearby neighborhood of Cambérène, which he often contrasted with the reasonable attitudes of members of his own neighborhood. He accused the people of Cambérène of unreasonably holding up the construction of the VDN 2 and causing problems for commuters on account of what he cast as their quirky belief that the state was out to harm them by building the VDN 2. He ridiculed them by claiming that

---

[5] I am using a pseudonym to ensure the anonymity of this research participant.

they could afford to scupper efforts to build the highway because they could always "visit their relatives in other Lébou villages along the littoral using their boats!"

The levels of trust that communities have in the state in Africa vary across space, leading to significant divergence in the outcomes of states' efforts to engage in development interventions across their national terrain. In explaining this variation in political trust, I go beyond literature that tended to homogenize the urban (Bates 1981; Bates 1993; Herbst 2000, 18) and rural spheres on the continent (Fallers 1961, 108–110; Hyden 1980; Zeleza 1993, 9–11; Bratton 1994; Herbst 2000; Lipton 2023). Like Hoelscher et al. (2023) and Paller (2019), I argue that there is diversity at the neighborhood level within the same urban area and that such variation has important causal implications for how state development interventions play out in urban areas. I argue that in Africa's colonial cities trust in the state is higher in neighborhoods dominated by recent migrants than in those that are predominantly populated by people claiming to be indigenous to these cities. Contestation, especially over land rights between these indigenous communities and the state dating back to the establishment of these cities has secreted a legacy of significant distrust of the state in indigenous neighborhoods that is absent in communities populated by more recent migrants. This makes it much harder for states to accomplish development interventions in these indigenous neighborhoods than in migrant ones in colonial cities.

The distinction between African cities with colonial origins and those whose creation and rise predated the colonial encounter with Europe is a problematic but analytically useful dichotomy employed by many scholars of African urbanism and history (Rayfield 1974; Sow 1983; King 1985; Southall 1989, 167–189; Coquery-Vidrovitch 1991, 1–98; Rakodi 1997, 24; Bocquier 2004, 134; Freund 2007; Sané 2013). I deploy it here as a scope condition. In Africa, the initial growth of cities with colonial origins unfolded under the control and regulation of European colonial authorities. These cities were often constructed in coastal areas (Bocquier 2004, 134) "to facilitate the extraction of commodities and the politico-administrative system on which this depended" (Rakodi 1997, 24). Dakar, Abidjan, Conakry, Brazzaville, and Luanda are all examples of these cities (Antoine and Savané 1990, 59; Herbst 2000, 16–17; Owuor and Mbatia 2012, 121; Tati 2012, 109). They differ from cities like Kumasi, Benin City, Harar, Abomey, Timbuktu, and Gao whose creation and development predated the continent's colonial encounter with Europe (Rayfield 1974; Hull 1976; Coquery-Vidrovitch 1993; Rakodi 1997, 19–25; Bocquire 2004, 133–134).

In cities born out of Africa's colonial experience, efforts by certain communities to gain recognition as autochthonous or indigenous owners of the lands on which these cities are constructed have pitted them in constant struggles against the colonial authorities and their postcolonial successors (La Fontaine 1970; Seck 1970; Vernier 1977; Diop 1993; Goerg 2006, 3–27; Onoma 2009; Sidibé 2015; Osseo-Asare 2016, 443–465; Njoh 2017). This contrasts with dynamics in cities that predated the colonial experience whose dominant indigenous elites and communities were acknowledged by the colonial and postcolonial authorities, including in situations where these state authorities have sought to curtail the power of these elites (Rayfield 1974, 173; Rathbone 2000; Boone 2003; Onoma 2009).

In postcolonial political contestations in Africa, the language of autochthony and indigeneity has been used frequently to separate those seen as properly belonging in certain spaces from "strangers" who are thought of as not really belonging there (Halisi, Kaiser, and Ndegwa 1998; Mamdani 2002; Geschiere 2009; Landau 2012; Onoma 2013; Nyamnjoh 2016; Boone 2017; Paller 2019; Onoma 2020; Hoelscher et al. 2023). The distinction often holds significance for rights to land, the ability to participate in political and economic life, standing before traditional legal systems, and even rights to a peaceful existence (Geschiere and Nyamnjoh 2000; Mamdani 2002; Onoma 2013; Boone 2017). The criteria invoked to separate "autochthones" from "strangers" are varied and multiple with people pointing to origination in a place, first arrival in a space, arrival before some other community and so on (Geschiere and Nyamnjoh 2000; Jackson 2006; Konings 2008; Onoma 2020). Debates over the timing of arrival and duration of stay in a space in these discourses are highly politicized as are the understandings of space (Murphy and Bledsoe 1987; Berry 2000; Jackson 2006). Far from being a self-evident, natural, and permanent characteristic, autochthony is a highly contested and tenuous quality requiring constant performance and continual defense.

Colonial authorities used various ruses to subvert the land claims of communities claiming autochthony in colonial cities. These authorities often portrayed the spaces chosen for the development of these cities as unoccupied and unowned spaces, or "empty, ownerless" lands, which they could legitimately take possession of (Suret-Canale 1971, 75; Njoh 2017). These authorities often tried to summarily expropriate, compulsorily acquire, purchase at disputed values, or use other ruses to seize large swathes of land in these spaces for urban development (Goerg 1989, 269–270; 1998, 20; 2006, 6; Njoh 2017). Postcolonial authorities have often followed in these footsteps (Onoma 2009, 129; Osseo-Asare 2016, 9; Njoh 2017). As land values have increased in these cities, land grabbing by well-placed postcolonial state officials for their personal economic and political benefits has been layered onto state expropriation and compulsory acquisition of lands for public purposes.

Autochthonous communities have seen these infringements on their land rights as illegitimate impositions and have resorted to resistance efforts that have included seeking judicial remedies, taking back and/or selling off lands acquired by the state, and demonstrating, including in violent ways, against these acquisitions (Georg 2006, 7; Sidibe 2015; Osseo-Asare 2016). Colonial and postcolonial state authorities, seeing these communities as "troublesome" have often further sidelined them in favor of collaboration with recent migrants to the city that state actors think of as more pliant (Goerg 1990, 75; 2006). For instance, in colonial Conakry, Guinea, the French authorities justified their imposition of new migrants to the city as chiefs by dismissing the local Baga and Soussou who claimed indigeneity in the area as "more or less drunkards and not to be taken seriously" (Goerg 2006, 12). It is often noted in the literature that these cities with colonial origins, unlike those that predate the colonial encounter, lack a dominant host community and are cosmopolitan (Pons 1969, 21; Rayfield 1974, 174; Onoma 2013). But the insistence on the "cosmopolitan" or "detribalized" character of these spaces by the colonial authorities was partly a deliberate effort to undermine these long-resident populations and cast these spaces as *terra nullius* – gathering spots for everyone but the property of none (Wright 1991, 303).

These struggles have left a legacy of very low trust in the state in these indigenous neighborhoods that has enhanced the tendency of these communities to challenge the state today. Over time, autochthonous communities have come to regard the development of these cities as having been at their expense (Goerg 2006, 7). Collective narratives, akin to Hur's "everyday oral histories that are shared informally and intimately among members" (Hur 2022, 21), are central to this process. These narratives that focus on dispossession, exploitation, and maltreatment by state authorities are passed down through generations and have, over time, become critical elements of the identities of these communities, creating a heightened distrust of the state. The state is often captured in these narratives of community identity and history as untrustworthy and dangerous. It is framed as an actor that communities must keep at arm's length. Where they are forced to interact with the state, they tend to counsel a defensive posture, close scrutiny and monitoring of state actions, and wariness of its mendacity. Frequent struggles against the state over land rights, going back to the founding of these colonial cities in the nineteenth century, have left a legacy of motivational narratives that encourage resistance to the state and its interventions.

Neighborhoods populated by newer migrants in these colonial cities demonstrate significantly higher levels of trust in the state on account of the state's central role in their ability to access land and housing. Unlike autochthonous communities in these cities, to whom the state has related as an expropriator of land rights, the state has related to these newer migrants as (potential) provider and/or formalizer of land rights. The state enticed some of these new city residents with land rights to settle in these cities to provide labor and undercut the domination of these cities by indigenous communities (La Fontaine 1970, 26–46; Riviere 1971, 29–40; Goerg 1990, 81–85; 1993, 90–99; 1998, 12; Fourchard 2009, 196–197). The state forcefully settled some of these newer residents in these cities to quell their rebellious behavior elsewhere or reward their support in wars (Goerg 1990, 77; Parsons 1997, 88–89; Goerg 2006, 11; Goerg 2012, 17; Balaton-Chrimes 2013, 338; Onoma 2013, 77; Elfversson and Höglund 2018, 3–4). Some who arrived in these cities on their own moved into new neighborhoods created or subsidized by the state or that they hoped would be regularized by the state in the future (Verniere 1977; Goerg 1998, 12; 2006, 15).

All of this ensures that distrust of the state and the insistence on wariness in interactions with it are not as central to the identities forged by these neighborhoods dominated by new migrants as they are to the identities of autochthonous neighborhoods. Instead, the narratives of community identity in these neighborhoods dominated by migrants often project the state as a (potential) creator or formalizer, even if an imperfect and not entirely reliable one, of their neighborhoods. In the face of challenges with accessing housing and a wide range of public services in many of these neighborhoods with high concentrations of recent migrants to these cities (Paller 2019), residents often project the state as a reluctant (future) savior to be wooed, urged, compelled, and even tricked into recognition of land rights and provision of related public goods. People in these neighborhoods trust the state and see its interventions as good, with residents all too often wondering how to attract and retain these interventions.

3.1 Neighborhood Identities and State Interventions

The capacity of the African state to undertake development interventions in these colonial cities takes an undulating form, rising and falling as it traverses neighborhoods that are dominated by autochthons and recent migrants on account of variations in levels of political trust across these communities. High levels of political trust make migrant neighborhoods more welcoming of state development interventions, obviating local resistance and enhancing the ability of the state to implement these projects. In autochthonous neighborhoods, low levels of political trust provoke local resistance that renders state implementation of these projects exceedingly challenging.

States' announcement of projects in communities that regard themselves as autochthonous in colonial cities elicits significant suspicion from the local community over the state's "real" intentions behind the project. People in these neighborhoods also raise concerns about the likelihood of the state using plans shared with them as cover to undertake projects that differ in significant ways from those outlined in the plans. Levi and Stoker (2000, 476) have noted how "distrust" "inspire[s] vigilance in and monitoring of a relationship, uncooperative behavior, or the severing of a relationship." Communities suspecting misleading discourses and a bait-and-switch strategy closely scrutinize state activities and incessantly contest various steps along the way, leading to significant delays in construction and the ballooning of budgets. Community members press for risk levels that are almost zero, with the understanding that the state will not be willing to remedy negative externalities that may arise in the future. This holds up the commencement of work on these infrastructure projects. These delays are exacerbated by the tendency to force the state to undertake risk reduction and offer inducements *before* undertaking work on the infrastructure project due to worries about the state reneging on commitments once its project is completed.

Similar announcements of state development interventions in communities that project themselves as melting pots of recent migrants elicit far less suspicion than in autochthonous neighborhoods about hidden state agendas that are harmful to their neighborhoods or a bait-and-switch strategy by the state. This obviates resistance to the commencement of these projects and ensures less effort to monitor and contest their implementation by the local community. Greater trust in the state also ensures that these neighborhoods are often more tolerant of risks associated with these projects, with many believing that the state will intervene in the future to deal with negative externalities that may arise. Trust in the state also influences their temporal horizons in the elimination of risks and the provision of inducements agreed upon with the state. They are more likely than their counterparts in autochthonous communities to agree to the state taking risk reduction measures and providing inducements *after* the completion of project implementation. Not insisting on inducements and risk reduction before project implementation facilitates the speedy completion of state interventions.

4 Cambérène: Intervening among Guarded Autochthons

The village of Cambérène was founded in 1887 by the Lébou sage and founder of the Layene Sufi Order, Seydina Limamou Laye. Worried about his iconoclastic messages and the throngs of followers from all over the Senegalese colony that he was attracting, the French colonial authorities forced Limamou Laye and his followers out of the Lébou village of Yoff on the outskirts of Dakar (Sylla 1971; Diagne 2011; Ross 2013). A 1911 map of Dakar indicates the location of the village that Limamou Laye and his followers created a short distance from where the village of Cambérène is located today.⁶ An elder in Cambérène informed us during an interview on July 3, 2019, that the village moved to its current location during the bubonic plague outbreak of 1914. This itinerant history and Cambérène's inclusion of people from all over Senegal are typical of many of the Lébou settlements in Dakar (Angrand 1946; Vernière 1977).

The population of Cambérène has grown steadily over time. A February 5, 1914, letter to the mayor of Dakar suggesting modifications to the boundaries of the city listed the population of Cambérène as 259.⁷ The population was listed as 2,000 in 1955 and 3,306 in 1970 (Vernière 1977, 45). By 2016, the population of Cambérène had grown to an estimated 57,302 (ANSD 2016). In 1996, the neighborhood was granted the status of a commune d'arrondissement (municipal district) in the Department of Dakar.

During an interview with a village leader and retired fisherman in Cambérène on July 3, 2019, he asserted that their neighborhood is an "autochthonous Lébou village like Yoff." This is a widely held view in the community that coincides with the thoughts of scholars who identify Cambérène and neighborhoods like Yoff, Ngor, Ouakam, and Hann as autochthonous Lébou communities in Dakar (Faure 1914; Angrand 1946; Mercier and Balandier 1953; Vernière 1977; Sylla 1992; Sidibé 2015). The Lébou, while vociferously claiming autochthony in Dakar (Angrand 1946; Sylla 1955; Sidibé 2013; 2015) often shy away from primordial understandings of identity and ideas of first arrival that sometimes mark discourses on autochthony (Geschiere and Nyamnjoh 2000; Jackson 2006; Geschiere 2009; Boone 2017). Lébou elders in Ngor (February 16, 2022), Ouakam, Yoff (February 23, 2022), and Cambérène (July 3, 2019) that I interviewed all stressed the important process of ethnogenesis among the Lébou that took place after the arrival of many migrating groups in the Cap Vert peninsula. These Lébou elders also emphasized their ancestors' deliberate creation of ties to the land upon their arrival in the peninsula through the establishment of relations with deities in the area that are reinforced today through rituals in Dakar (Also see Sidibé 2013; Angrand 1946). In addition to this spiritual work, the Lébou also invoked their long-standing efforts to defend these rights they had secured to land in the peninsula from various adversaries. These narratives accord with accounts of many scholars of the history of the Cap Vert Peninsular where Dakar is located and Senegal (Faure 1914; Angrand 1946;

---

⁶ See folder 11D1.1282 (Archives Nationales du Sénégal).
⁷ See folder 11D3/14: Dakar et Banlieu Rufisque (Archives Nationales du Sénégal).

Mercier and Balandier 1952; Sylla 1955; Vernière 1977; Diouf 1990; Sylla 1992; Sidibé 2013).

Before the arrival of the French colonizers, the Damel (ruler) of the precolonial Kingdom of Cayor represented the principal threat to the rights of Lébou communities in the Cap Vert peninsula. The rulers of Cayor claimed the peninsula as part of their kingdom and saw the lands there as their domain, with which they could do as they wished (Angrand 1946; Sylla 1955; Diouf 1990). Lébou communities resented and over time came to reject these claims. Their military resistance to the impositions of the rulers of Cayor in the early 1790s culminated in a formal peace pact with and recognition of their independent "Lébou Republic" in 1812 by the rulers of Cayor (Faure 1914, 50; Angrand 1946, 53; Sylla 1955, 41; Diouf 1990).

4.1 The Arrival of a New Adversary

It was in 1857, forty-five years after this peace pact with Cayor, that Captain Auguste Léopold Protet, commander of the French Naval Division of the West Coast of Africa, founded a French colony in Dakar by landing a boatload of French marines from the nearby island of Gorée (Sylla 1955; Jost 1968; Seck 1970; Bouche 1978, 423). After the French admiral Jean d'Estrées took over Gorée in 1677, the island served, with only few interruptions by the British, as a major center of the French trading and bourgeoning colonial enterprise in West Africa (Frewen 1897; Camara and de Benoist 2003, 18; de Benoist 2008, 88). As French ambitions in West Africa grew the issue of a capital befitting the sprawling project envisioned arose as the limitations of Gorée due to its insular character and small size became apparent (Faure 1914, 8).

Across the water from Gorée lay Dakar, on which the people of Gorée had for long depended for food, fresh water, and building materials (Faure 1914, 13, 101; Angrand 1946, 68–82). It was a larger space and offered great commercial possibilities (Faure 1914, 101–119; Angrand 1946, 83–84). Protet's landing in 1857 was the culmination of a long debate among French officials, some of whom had for long touted what they saw as the extraordinary promise of the site (Faure 1914). After a short period of stagnation, the new colony in Dakar grew rapidly in size, population, and importance (Vernière 1977, 16; Khouma 2007, 57; Sané 2013, 313). Its modest population of 1,556 in 1878 (Jost 1968, 50) grew to 8,700 in 1900 (M'Bokolo 1982, 15), 18,000 in 1904 (Jost 1968, 50; M'Bokolo 1982, 15), 30,000 in 1907 (M'Bokolo 1982, 15), over 400,000 in 1965 (Seck 1968, 17), and around 1,252,786 in 2016 (ANSD 2016, 8). In 1902 Dakar was named the capital of Afrique-Occidentale française, a federation of eight French colonies (Seck 1970, 296) and in 1958 it became the capital of the colony of Senegal (Seck 1970, 296; Diop 2012, 33).

The creation of a French colony in Dakar transformed the colonial administration into the new principal adversary of the Lébou and created unceasing conflict over land rights between the two, akin to that seen between colonizers and indigenous populations in other colonial cities on the continent (Angrand 1946; Sylla 1955; La Fontaine 1970; Suret-Canale 1971; Georg 1989; Fourchard 2009; Sidibé 2015; Njoh 2017). Having only recently liberated themselves from the domination of Cayor, the Lébou were particularly protective of their autonomy and land rights when the French arrived in the peninsula. The then administrator of Senegal, Colonel Julien-Désiré Schmaltz, had foreseen this earlier in 1817 when he warned that "with their sense of pride inflated by their success against the Damel whose yoke they have completely thrown off, they [the Lébou] have become insolent and over demanding" (Faure 1914, 36).

Facing the Lébou was a French colonial administration that believed, to use the emphatic 1857 words of the French Minister of the Navy and the Colonies, Ferdinand Alphonse Hameline, that Dakar was "a place that is ours."[8] The first urban development plan, shown in Figure 3, which was drawn by the military engineer Émile Pinet-Laprade in July 1862, assumed that the area was a void on which the French could build the city they wished (Jost 1968, 51; Seck 1970, 273–274). The neat checkerboard plan of the city drawn by Pinet-Laprade five years after the arrival of the French there ignored both the existence and layout of the Lébou settlements in the part of the Cap Vert Peninsula that the French had chosen for their new colonial city (Calvet and Ragon 1982, 23).

Pinet-Laprade's map was an early indication of the French determination to seize the lands in the peninsula that they wanted for their new city. The French initially laid claims to lands in the peninsula based on supposed treaties with the rulers of Cayor in the 1600s and 1700s, as well as their military defeat of the kingdom (Angrand 1946, 68–99; Seck 1970, 273–274). The Lébou countered these arguments by pointing out that the rulers of Cayor never had control or ownership of lands in the Cap Vert peninsula, rendering their treaties with or defeat by the French irrelevant for land claims in the peninsula (Seck 1970, 273). Undeterred, Governor Jaureguibery's February 28, 1862, decree persisted in equating lands in Dakar to those in the Kingdom of Cayor and banned the Lébou from alienating land in the peninsula (Angrand 1946, 97). Retracting only slightly in the face of Lébou complaints, a commission

---

[8] L9: Fondation et acquisition de terrains à Dakar (Archives nationales du Sénégal). Letter from The Minister of the Navy and the Colonies on June 16, 1857, to the Commander of the Station on the West Coast of Africa.

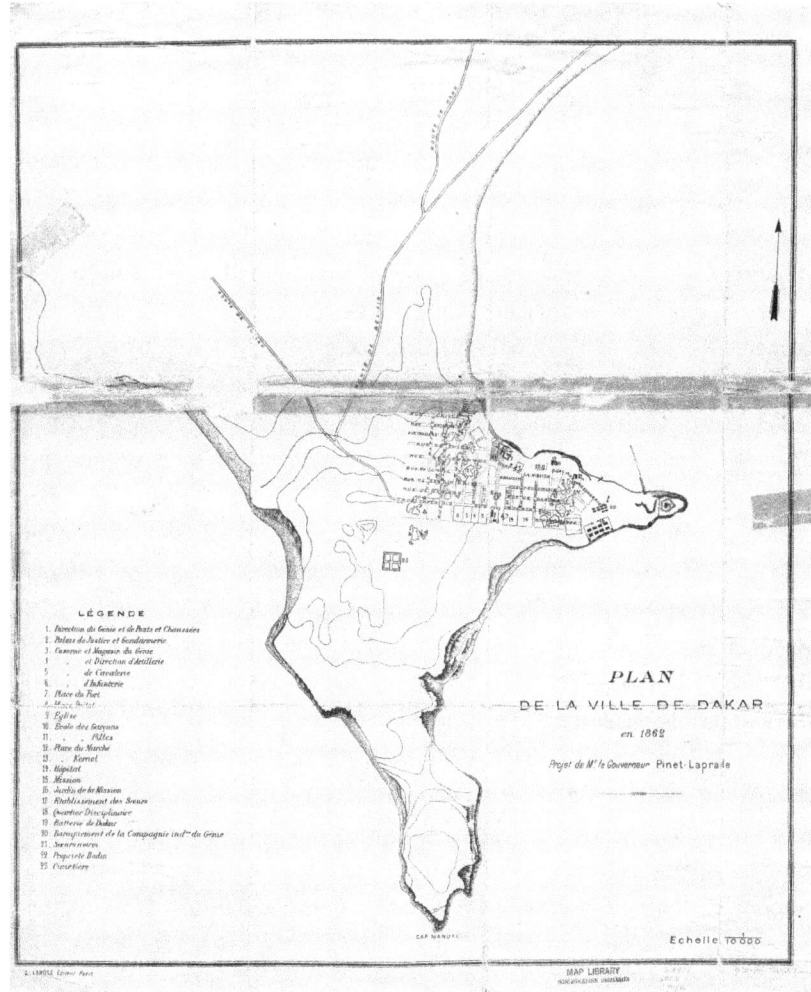

Figure 3 Plan of the city of Dakar in 1862.
Source: Image courtesy of the Melville J. Herskovits Library of African Studies, Northwestern University Libraries.

established by the French authorities in 1889 asserted the right of the state to take over all untitled lands in the peninsula in its 1891 report (Angrand 1946, 104), echoing similar claims over "empty, ownerless" lands by colonial authorities around the world (Suret-Canale 1971; Coquery-Vidrovitch 1972; Berry 2002; Tuori 2015).

To meet the rising demand for land from government agencies and private enterprises alike, the French employed a combination of subterfuge and force to gradually push the Lébou out of their long-established villages near the new

French settlement (Seck 1970, 128; Sylla 1991; Diop 1993).[9] The French imposed construction regulations that made it impossible for many Lébou to stay in their old villages (Angrand 1946, 100–103; Ndiaye 2015, 52). A June 1, 1859, proclamation by Pinet-Laprade, giving the state the right to take all lands required for public road construction and realignment as long as those lands did not belong to the people of Gorée (Clavet and Ragon n.d., 20–21), forced even more Lébou out of their villages (Angrand 1946, 100–101). The colonial authorities also used the cover of epidemic control and prevention to expel Lébou communities from lands close to the city center (Seck 1970, 129; Vernière 1977, 25; M'Bokolo 1982; Echenberg 2002; Ndiaye 2015, 52).[10] In 1905 the French took over two massive parcels of land – the Bougnoul and Tound – with compensation, continuing a gradual process of coercive acquisition with compensation that had started from the early days of the city's existence (Seck 1970, 122–125; Diop 1993, 48).[11]

Akin to struggles by autochthonous communities facing similar expropriation of their land rights in other colonial cities on the continent (Suret-Canale 1971; Onoma 2013; Njoh 2017), the Lébou waged a trenchant struggle in the face of these colonial efforts to usurp their land rights (Seck 1970, 128; Vernière 1977, 40; Sylla 1992; Diop 1993, 51). They denounced and submitted multiple petitions against these measures in addition to seeking judicial remedies where possible (Angrand 1946, 104, 114; Seck 1970, 128; Vernière 1977, 40; M'Bokolo 1982, 41; Sylla 1992; Diop 1993, 51). They also demonstrated and even occasionally violently resisted this usurpation of their rights. When the colonial authorities tried to burn the homes of Lébou villagers and expel them from their villages in the name of epidemic control and prevention during the 1914 plague epidemic in Dakar, livid armed members of the community violently confronted colonial troops (Angrand 1946, 126; M'Bokolo 1982, 41–42; Echenberg 2002, 60).

In an example of what Ndlovu-Gatsheni has referred to as the "coloniality of power in postcolonial Africa" (Ndlovu-Gatsheni 2013), the postcolonial Senegalese state continued the colonial practice of forcefully evicting marginal

---

[9] See the minutes of a meeting of the Commission established to study the steps to be taken for the construction of new roads and public buildings on March 3, 1904. P167: Urbanisme Dakar 1901–1918 (Archives nationales du Sénégal). Also see report prepared by the Head of Military Works dated November 29, 1901, in the same folder. Further, L9: Fondation et acquisition de terrains à Dakar (Archives nationales du Sénégal) contains diverse letters from businesses requesting land in Dakar and responses by colonial officials to these requests.

[10] See multiple documents concerning the creation of Medina in the folder ANS 11D1.1284: Nouveau village indigène de Dakar (Archives nationales du Sénégal).

[11] L9: Fondation et acquisition de terrains à Dakar (Archives nationales du Sénégal). See official documents on land acquisitions in Dakar by the colonial administration in the early days of the colony.

communities, including the Lébou, from "slums" close to the ever-expanding city center to settle them in increasingly more remote outlying areas (Vernière 1977, 28–33). This process of dispossession and removal in Dakar, as in other metropolises around the world (Bob-Milliar and Obeng-Odoom 2011; Weinstein 2013; Njoh 2017; Kwak 2018; Paller 2019; Di Nunzio 2022) has led to the further marginalization of vulnerable communities in the name of urban redevelopment and renewal. The state's Loi de la domaine nationale of 1964, continued the annexation of Lébou lands in transferring ownership in all unregistered lands in the country to the state (Vernière 1977, 41; Diop 1993, 41–50; Sidibé 2013; Sidibé 2015).

The uses of Lébou lands appropriated by the state go beyond official projects. As in many African countries (Onoma 2009; Osseo-Asare 2016; Boone 2017; Njoh 2017; Paller 2019), struggles over land rights are pervasive in Senegal today and the resource occupies an important place in national and local democratic politics. It is a big motivator for political activism, an important resource for rewarding allies and buying the support of influential actors, and a great means of mobilizing money for uses that include political campaigns (Faye et al. 2011; Sow 2013; Touré and Seck 2013; Faye 2015; Ndiaye T. 2020a; Ndiaye T. 2020b). Since the year 2000, there has been a wave of land grabbing by politically influential actors in the city targeting the lands of important state institutions and the city's seafront that is protected as a Domaine Public Maritime (Sidibé 2013; 2015; Fall 2015; Diagne 2020; Gueye 2020; Le Quotidien 2020; Niakar 2020; Sall 2020; Seye 2022; Ndiaye T. 2024b; Sy, Diallo, and Kane 2009).

The take-over of lands initially acquired by the state for public purposes by well-connected individuals has only further vexed Lébou communities, who think the state should instead return lands no longer needed for the public good to them (Sidibé 2013; Diallo 2016; Niakar 2020; Seye 2022). The Lébou continued the long struggle to defend their land rights that had previously pitted them in battles against the rulers of Cayor and the French colonial authorities through the release of communiques, demonstrations, and violent revolts that sometimes resulted in significant damage to property and loss of lives (Bonhoure 2015; Diallo 2016; Le Quotidien 2020a; Niakaar 2020; Kiennemann 2023).

4.2 The Challenge of Intervening in an Adversarial Context

The stylized narratives that anchor communal identities, which scholars like Hur (2022) and Bouchard (2013) discuss, are pervasive in Lébou communities. These narratives center on long-standing struggles against the colonial and postcolonial state over land rights and are passed down through generations (Sidibé 2015). They emphasize historical Lébou losses to, and continual victimization at, the hands of the Senegalese state. They cast the state as an untrustworthy institution that is best kept at arm's length. When interactions are deemed absolutely necessary, these narratives counsel the careful surveillance of the state to ensure the community is protected from what are cast as its almost inevitably harmful actions (Sidibé 2013; 2015).

The drastically low level of trust in the state within these communities has created a chasm between Lébou villages in Dakar and national and municipal authorities tasked with both routine administrative tasks and major development projects. Lébou communities have not always been willing to collaborate with the state on interventions in their communities (Sidibé 2015). They often seek to place themselves "outside of the legal and regulatory systems in place in Senegal and the city [of Dakar]" (Sidibé 2015, 25). Lébou property holders, for instance, often insist that the state should not subject their lands to documentation rules because "the land is theirs" as autochthones of the peninsula (Sidibé 2015, 25). They have created parallel land management systems to shield themselves from what they cast as the depredations of the state (Ndiaye 2015), thereby subverting state efforts to create a comprehensive cadaster.

Even when they regard state projects and interventions as vital for their communal wellbeing, Lébou communities tend to be extremely guarded and approach these interactions with acute suspicion. As I spoke to people in Cambérène during research for this project, I noticed that they tended to think that, like onions, state interventions have multiple layers and that if you kept peeling long enough, you were sure to uncover a sinister plan of some sort. The Lébou display a marked skepticism over state discourses about national development and how various projects fit into this process (Sidibé 2013; 2015, 25). This has led to significant hesitancy on their part to collaborate with the state, even on those projects that they [the Lébou] desire. The link between "distrust" and "vigilance in and monitoring of a relationship, uncooperative behavior, or the severing of a relationship," highlighted by Levi and Stoker (2000, 476), is apparent in these interactions. The Lébou closely scrutinize and monitor state projects and incessantly contest "deviations" that they see as contrary to agreed-upon plans (Sidibé 2015). As in other cases of infrastructure development (Dear 1992; Schively 2007; Einstein, Glick, and Palmer 2020; Foster and Warren 2022), this guardedness has sometimes secured local community interests and improved the design and delivery of infrastructure. As pointed out by scholars focusing on other contexts (Hyden 1980; Scott 1999), such guardedness has also often raised the cost of these interventions and doomed many to complete failure.

State and municipal officials, frustrated by what they regard as the overly adversarial and confrontational attitude of the Lébou, sometimes refrain from even beginning to engage these neighborhoods on certain projects implemented in the rest of the city or to carry out routine administrative tasks there. These officials argue that "dealing with community tensions and arriving at a consensus with them [the Lébou] is too difficult" (Sidibé 2015, 29). A building inspector from the state's Urban Development Directorate, who admitted that they often shy away from inspecting new constructions in Lébou villages, indicated that they "prefer to close [their] eyes than to fight against an entire neighborhood. The Lébou are powerful because they are united. They are autochthones that have a reputation for being boorish" (Sidibé 2015, 25).

The exceedingly low level of trust in the state within Lébou communities influenced how residents of Cambérène reacted to the state's VDN 2 project. Many of those interviewed for this study in Cambérène tended not to take the state's broad narrative about the importance of the VDN 2 to "*l'émergence du pays*" at face value. Many were convinced that the highway project was at least partly a façade for something more menacing or that the state was likely to switch plans to something more sinister once it secured the approval of the community. There was a particularly strong suspicion that the state was going to use the highway to cut the community off from the seafront to facilitate the grabbing of coastal land by the rich and powerful. The refrain "they [state authorities] are not telling us the whole truth" was one that I heard often in discussions with people in the neighborhood. People brought up the history of Lébou losses at the hands of the state. They often cited the frenzied grabbing of lands on the city's Corniche West, Ouakam, and Ngor by shady figures connected to those in power that marked the rule of Macky Sall (Sy, Diallo, and Kane 2009). Scholars have noted this dampening effect of low political trust on locals' attitudes toward state interventions in other contexts (Dear 1992, 292; Gibson 2005, 382; Obadare 2005; Hutchison and Johnson 2017).

"Why should we believe all that they are telling us about this road?" asked the leader of one of the main organizations that contested the state's effort to undertake the VDN 2 project along the coast of Cambérène during an interview on July 10, 2018 (Interview 1). This question, which casts distrust of the state as normal, reflected similar sentiments expressed by other leading members of community organizations in Cambérène. An old veteran of earlier contestations of state interventions, who acted as an advisor to the leaders of one of the groups actively contesting the state's construction plans, expressed similar sentiments during a July 10, 2018 interview.

> People are spreading rumors about us [the inhabitants of Cambérène] saying we don't want a road and that we are against the development of the country, but it is all false. It is just that we want them to listen to our ideas. We also want to make sure they are telling us the entire truth behind this project. (Interview 4)

An active member of one of the groups, in a July 10, 2018, interview in Cambérène, re-echoed this distrust in the state's broad narrative and suspicions of a bait-and-switch strategy in its interactions with the community:

> People [in the rest of the city] are saying many bad things about us [the inhabitants of Cambérène] but most of them are lies. We do not have anything against the government or the construction of a road. But we do have problems with how they want to build this road. And we also know that the authorities are not telling us all the truth. What they say they are going to do and what they are actually trying to do on the ground here are diametrically opposed. (Interview 2)

The impact of the lack of political trust on local attitudes towards risks presented by infrastructure projects, as discussed in the literature (Schively 2007; Wang et al. 2021) was evident in how residents of Cambérène approached negotiations with the state over the VDN construction project. Not counting on the state to help them deal with the negative externalities of the highway in the future, they aggressively pushed for a design that reduced risks to almost zero. They sought a design that would not involve people crossing the highway to reach or surveil the beach they use on a quotidian basis for fishing, leisure, sports, and rituals. Community members made no secret of their unwillingness to compromise on their demands for a zero-risk design. The leader of one of the associations involved in struggles with the state, Le Comité d'initiative pour la défense de l'environnement de Cambérène, boldly proclaimed to journalists that "no concessions will be made" in its discussions with the state on the design and implementation of the project (Agence de Presse Sénégalaise 2018a).

Lacking trust in the state to fulfill promises made during these exchanges, the people of Cambérène were adamant that risk reduction measures and inducements promised by the state be delivered *before* construction on the highway began. The movement leader cited above (Interview 1) listed their demands during an interview on October 7, 2018: jobs for youth in the neighborhood, streetlights, improved access to pipe-borne water, better sewage and drainage systems, and construction of public spaces and places of leisure. Given the nature of these demands, their completion before the commencement of road construction was bound to significantly delay the implementation of the highway project. Community members even forced the state to build a bowstring bridge over a segment of the highway to ensure the highway did not cut off the mausoleum of the late Layenne leader, Seydina Issa Rohou Lahi, from the sea (DakarActu 2018).

The tendency of activist groups and community organizations to meticulously surveil work on the construction site and contest what they saw as deviations from the plan the state had shared with the community severely delayed construction. It led to frequent stoppages of work and occasionally even resulted in the destruction of structures that the builders had constructed. This fixation on monitoring construction work was fueled by suspicion that the state was trying to implement something other than the plan it had shared with the community.

The two-page minutes of a May 2, 2019, meeting, one of the many held between community leaders and Ageroute SN officials, provide some evidence of this preoccupation of community members with surveilling and monitoring what they saw as an untrustworthy state.[12] The first joint decision of the convening that is noted in the minutes is that "The plans that Ageroute presented to the authorities in Cambérène will be effectively implemented," betraying community members' strong suspicion of a bait-and-switch strategy by the state. This was not the only aspect of the minutes that betrayed an intent to keep the state on the straight and narrow path. The preliminary remarks in the minutes state an agreement to create a "consultation framework that will meet periodically," with the monitoring of ongoing work as a priority. The minutes return to this question of monitoring again in the list of decisions, stating in point three that "A very supple monitoring and consultation committee will be created that will ensure the periodic monitoring of the implementation of plans agreed on." To further avoid ambiguities, the minutes even included specific measurements of the size and heights of aspects of the highway to be constructed through the neighborhood, which would presumably be the subject of monitoring by these mechanisms!

Even though Cambérène was part of the Plateforme des riverains de la VDN that brought together all the communities affected by the VDN 2, community members almost exclusively channeled their activism through a panoply of structures operating exclusively in their neighborhood. Some of these organizations, like the Collectif des Riverains Impactés de la VDN 2 à Cambérène, Cambérène Mognou Nior (Cambérène is our priority), and Cambérène Sama Gox (Cambérène my neighborhood), were created to engage the state and its constructor on the VDN 2 project. Others, like the Comité d'initiative pour la défense de l'environnement de Cambérène, were organizations that predated the VDN project and were created during earlier rounds of contesting state interventions (Agence de Presse Sénégalaise 2018a). While many of these organizations spoke on behalf of the whole community, some were more focused on the interests of segments of the community. The Association des pêcheurs de Cambérène, for instance, sought to get the state to offset the

---

[12] "Compte rendu de réunion," minutes of a meeting held at the offices of Ageroute SN from 10:30am on May 2, 2019, between officials of Ageroute and leaders from Cambérène on "the modalities to restart work on the VDN 2 at Cambérène." My translations from the original French.

negative externalities of the highway and its construction process on fishermen's livelihoods (Le Quotidien 2018).

These groups sometimes collaborated in their activities, and many individuals belonged to and participated in the activities of multiple organizations. At other times, they competed against each other for the right to speak on behalf of the community, with some publicly undercutting others (Le Quotidien 2020b; Ndiaye, T. M. 2020). The competition and contestation between these groups reflect long histories of contestation within the Lébou community over the right to represent the community, along with the benefits and rewards that come with it (M'Bokolo 1982, 37; Bocoum 2013; Gueye 2013).[13] These intra-communal contestations reinforce criticism of the tendency to cast local communities confronting states as internally homogenous, placid and even harmonious (Chattarjee 2004; Dill 2013; Paller 2019).

The youth in Cambérène were the most active and visible participants in these movements, reflecting the wide role that youth have come to play in struggles over human rights, political and economic reform, and the provision of public goods on the continent (Honwana 2012; Bob-Milliar 2014; Branch and Mampilly 2015; Dimé 2017; Van Gyampo and Anyidoho 2019; Dimé et al. 2021). During interviews, some of the leaders of these organizations stressed the political work of building awareness in the community and mobilizing youth to take part in demonstrations, echoing the emphasis on the role of networks in contemporary urban contestation by Pasotti (2020) and Kwak (2018). Activists created links with other community associations and organizations partly by incorporating their leaders. It is in this regard that the head of one of the leading koranic schools in the neighborhood that we interviewed on July 10, 2018 (Interview 6) got integrated into and became an active member of one of these activist movements. Using her links with parents whose children attended her school and her influence in the community, she was able to sensitize and mobilize many in the neighborhood for the cause.

Contestation of the project came to a head in early 2018 when community members noticed the construction of a massive bridge ramp on the beach. For many in the community, "The wall of shame," "The wall of discord," or "The Berlin wall," as the structure came to be variously called (Xalimasn 2018) confirmed long-standing fears that the state had a hidden plan to cut their neighborhood

---

[13] The Archives nationales du Sénégal contains information on these contestations. For instance, the Delegate of the Governor of Senegal sent a letter to the Governor on October 7, 1923, denouncing a move by some Lébou notables to remove El Hadj Moussé Diop from the prestigious and powerful position of Grand Serigne of Dakar only five months after he assumed that office with the dispute partly involving disagreements over the sharing of compensation for lands taken over by the state. 11D3/14: Dakar et Banlieu Rufisque (Archives nationales du Sénégal).

off from the beach. People embarked on what popularly came to be known among activists as the "revolt against the construction of the wall." It involved a wave of social media activism, press conferences, demonstrations, disruptions of traffic in the area, invasions of the construction site, and seizure of construction equipment that brought construction to a halt as workers stayed away for their safety (Ndiaye A. 2018; Ndiaye F. 2018a; Xalimasn 2018; Nettali 2019). This created a gap in the otherwise completed highway that is shown in Figure 4.

The state partly responded to these disruptions by deploying detachments of police and gendarmes to reopen blockaded roads and protect construction equipment. High-level state officials also met with community representatives and agreed to implement many of the changes they demanded, including the complete demolition of "the wall" and its replacement with an elevated highway that allowed villagers unimpeded access to the beach (Dieng 2018; Ndiaye, F. 2018a). Constructors spent months destroying "the wall" in late 2018. They then briefly restarted work on the highway in early 2019 before abandoning work altogether in the face of further community contestation. Construction recommenced in late 2020, and the segment of the highway there was completed and opened to traffic only in March 2022, three years after motorists started using the rest of the VDN 2.

Speaking to journalists, a state official involved in the highway construction project indicated that the stop-and-go process, as well as the destruction and reconstruction of segments of the road, had significantly raised construction

Figure 4 The VDN 2 drops into an abyss at Cambérène in June 2019.

costs, forcing the state to seek additional funds to complete the highway (Gaye 2018; Ndiaye F. 2018a). Dynamics during the VDN 2 construction constitute just another instance of community members in these autochthonous neighborhoods protecting themselves, sometimes at great cost to the community, from what they see as an untrustworthy state and its interventions.

5 Parcelles Assainies: Highway Construction in a "New" Neighborhood

In both its 2016 and 2018 official guides, the Commune of Parcelles Assainies in Dakar proudly touts itself as a new neighborhood that is "very heterogenous in terms of ethnicity" (Commune de Parcelles Assainies 2016, 6; Commune de Parcelles Assainies 2018, 11). This identity as a melting pot of recent migrants from around Senegal and elsewhere in West Africa, within the colonial city of Dakar, has resulted in high levels of political trust among neighborhood residents. This greater trust in the state motivated the embrace of the state's VDN 2 project by residents and enhanced the state's capacity to construct the segment of the highway that passes along the neighborhood's coast.

Parcelles Assainies is part of what Vernière (1977, 11) calls "ex nihilo" creations to cater for a rapidly rising urban population in Dakar. The city's galloping population after the turn of the twentieth century was largely due to migrant inflows (Mbacké, Ndao, and Ndonky 2024). The concentration of opportunities and services in cities, which has fueled rural-urban migration in many African contexts (Byerlee 1974; Bekker and Therborn 2012) encouraged many from other areas of the French colony to come to the city (Vernière 1977; Diop 2012; Sané 2013). Dakar's status as the capital of Afrique-Occidentale française also helped it attract migrants from other colonies in the federation (Sow 1983, 46–47). Significant populations from areas farther afield that have settled in Dakar include Lebanese, Syrians, Europeans, especially French, Cape Verdians, and Moroccans (O'Brien 1972; Vernière 1977; M'Bokolo 1982).

The thorny question of housing rapidly rising urban populations, which has bedeviled many cities around the world (Njoh 2013; Okeyinka 2014; Paller 2015; Wakely 2018; Favilukis, Mabille, and Van Nieuwerburgh 2023) has over time preoccupied both the colonial administration and the postcolonial state that succeeded it in Senegal. Like in other African contexts (Njoh 2013), the Senegalese state has adopted what Sané (2013, 315) referred to as a "dirigiste housing policy," installing the state as a leading provider of houses and land to the residents of Dakar. Goerg, notes that "French colonial cities welcomed mixed populations offering free access to land" to urbanites (Goerg 1998, 2). The lands that were so dispensed to new arrivals in Dakar by the colonial and postcolonial authorities were those acquired in coercive ways from the Lébou who are Indigenous to the city. Like dynamics in other colonial cities (Pons 1969; Rayfield 1974; Wright 1991; Njoh 2013; Onoma 2013; Njoh 2017) the gains of the new arrivals in Dakar were in essence the losses of autochthonous Lébou communities. These diverging relations with the state have influenced levels of political trust and attitudes toward state developmental interventions across the city.

5.1 Housing "New" Dakarois: the Parcelles Assainies Project

The Senegalese state's provision of housing and furnishing of support to others developing housing in Dakar is facilitated by a plethora of ministries, agencies, directorates, and laws. By 2012, there were at least twelve state directorates and multiple ministries for whom the provision of housing and support for providers of housing was a major preoccupation (ONU Habitat 2012, 28). The work of these agencies is facilitated by a multitude of legal instruments, with the most important being the Law of the National Domain (Law No. 64 of June 1964), which rendered all undocumented lands in the country part of a national domain administered by the state. Related to this is the Code of the State Domain (Law 76–66 of July 1976), which regulates lands that are considered to properly belong to the state. An important part of this law is its provision for a public maritime domain (Domaine Public Maritime), which is particularly important to development in the city of Dakar, as it is almost surrounded by the Atlantic Ocean. There is also the Urbanism Code (Law No. 64–49 of July 1966, replaced by new codes in 1988 and 2008) that regulates urban development. The Law No. 76–67 of July 1976, which deals with expropriations for public utility, is similarly relevant here (ONU Habitat 2012, 25).

Two state housing agencies have stood out in the work of translating these and other policy instruments into housing for Dakar's booming population. The state first established the Société Immobilière du Cap-Vert (SICAP) in 1952 (Sané 2013, 316). Then, in 1959, it created the Office des Habitations à Loyer Modéré (OHLM), which was subsequently renamed Société Nationale des Habitations à Loyer Modéré (SN-HLM) in 1997. These two institutions have constructed and delivered houses to people in Dakar through lease-purchase arrangements. Between 1951 and 1997, SICAP built and delivered an average of 250 houses a year (White 1985, 511), while SN-HLM built, on average, 335 houses a year over its first 40 years of existence (ONU Habitat 2012, 2). The activities of both parastatals are concentrated in Dakar, given the exceedingly high demand for housing there. The exclusion of the poor in the offerings of state housing parastatals that Njoh (2013) notes in Cameroon is also present in

Dakar. The activities of SICAP and SN-HLM have largely excluded poorer Senegalese. SICAP has focused on the upper echelons of the bureaucracy and wealthy classes, while SN-HLM has targeted the middle and working classes in Senegalese society (Sow 1983, 48; Sané 2013, 316). Housing estates constructed by these entities proliferate in the city and include those at Fann Hock, Fann-Résidence, Point E, Zone B, Mermoz, Sacré-Cœur, Amitié 1, Amitié 2, Amitié 3, and Karak-Baobab. To this list, we can add the estates of Liberté 1, Liberté 2, Liberté 3, Liberté 4, Liberté 5, Liberté 6, Dieuppeul 1, Dieuppeul 2, Dieuppeul 3, and HLM 1, HLM 2, HLM 3, HLM 4, HLM 5, and HLM 6 (Calvet and Ragon 1982, 33–36).

The need to accelerate housing delivery in the face of galloping urbanization led the state, very early on, to adopt the strategy of furnishing free or highly subsidized land parcels on which people could build their own houses. Multiple estates in Pikine, Guédiawaye, Keur Massa, Malika, and Mbao are results of this effort (Vernière 1973; Sow 1983; ONU Habitat 2012; Sané 2013). SN-HLM delivered an average of 570 serviced parcels a year over the first 40 years of its existence (ONU Habitat 2012, 2). To further boost the speed with which land and houses were delivered, the state has over time created ephemeral structures to provide land and houses to the urban population. These include Société des habitations modernes (HAMO) (1981–1990) and Société Centrale d'aménagement des terrains urbains (SCAT-URBAM) (Sané 2013, 317–318).

In the Cap Vert peninsula, marked by rapid immigration, settlements have often outpaced efforts by the state to provide houses and land. This means that, like authorities elsewhere in the Global South (Handzic 2010; Wakely 2018), the Senegalese state has sometimes resorted to "regularizing" rights to lands that have already been occupied and to "restructuring" already established neighborhoods. Between 1991 and 2010, Fondation Droit à la Ville, a private not-for-profit foundation that the state partnered with regularized around 6,469 parcels in the city and its outskirts (ONU Habitat 2012, 2, 18; Sané 2013, 326–327). Beyond providing land and houses directly to urban dwellers, the Senegalese state has aided private developers and cooperatives in developing housing in Dakar by making land and financing accessible to them (Sané 2013, 321). The state created the Bureau d'Assistance aux Collectivités pour l'Habitat Social (BAHSO) to help cooperatives access land and provide technical support to those seeking to provide housing. It also created the Banque de l'Habitat du Sénégal (BHS) to provide favorable loans to cooperatives and private developers (ONU Habitat 2012, 21).

The creation of the neighborhood of Parcelles Assainies was part of the state's effort to provide affordable housing for the rapidly increasing population of Dakar.

The central role of the state and its officials in the creation of the neighborhood mirrors the key part that the state has played in settling new migrants in other colonial cities in Africa (La Fontaine 1970; Riviere 1971; Georg 1998; Fourchard 2009; Onoma 2013; Elfversson and Höglund 2018). The creation of Parcelles Assainies commenced in 1972 when the government of Senegal, with funding from the World Bank set about creating a site-and-service scheme on 400 acres of coastal land lying between the Lébou villages of Cambérène and Yoff (Tall 1994, 141; White 1985, 505–528; Sané 2013, 320; World Bank 2015, 57). OHLM demarcated and serviced 10,500 plots in 20 neighborhoods known as "Units" in the scheme (ONU Habitat 2012, 16; Commune de Parcelles Assainies 2018, 11). Applicants for plots in the estate were supposed to demonstrate their ability to develop the parcel as well as show that their earnings were under the ceiling set by the state. Parcelles Assainies grew to become one of the most densely populated neighborhoods in Dakar with a population of 174,352 in 2016 (ANSD 2016, 514). It was made into a commune d'arrondisement in 1996 (Commune de Parcelles Assainies 2018, 11).

Engagement with specific state bureaucrats at a personal level was often critical to people's ability to access plots in Parcelles Assainies. It was relatives, friends, or acquaintances who were state officials who informed some of the opportunity to acquire plots in Parcelles Assainies and guided them through what was a complicated application process (White 1985, 513–518). Some exploited links with officials serving on the committee that attributed plots to get the specific parcels they desired, to obtain multiple parcels for speculative purposes, to acquire plots despite their income far surpassing the ceiling set by the state, and to acquire parcels even though they were already beneficiaries of houses in other state housing schemes (Sarr 1984, 10; White 1985, 518). In a further boost to plot recipients, the state provided those it judged in need of assistance with construction loans beginning in 1976. It doubled the size of these loans in 1978, deeming the initial amount to be insufficient (Sarr 1984, 10).

The role of the state in the origination of Parcelles Assainies has guaranteed it a prominent and positive status of neighborhood creator in the enunciations of communal history and identity by residents of Parcelles Assainies. Residents of the neighborhood express significant trust in the state and view it as an actor that plays a positive role in society. This recognition of the state's creative role, which people emphasize in new neighborhoods like Parcelles Assainies, is rooted in the intersection between the importance of acquiring housing for new urban residents and the difficulty of achieving this for many of them (Chatterjee 2004; Paller 2015; Kwak 2018; Paller 2019; Di Nunzio 2022). Acquiring a house or land has for long been one of the greatest desires of new arrivals in cities (Sow 1983; Wakely 2018). In addition to alleviating a fundamental need that many in the city face, it serves as a signal of success and assimilation into the new urban environment (Vernière 1973, 226; Sané 2013, 316–317). In Dakar there was always a high number of people seeking housing that is provided or subsidized by state agencies. When Parcelles Assainies was created in 1972, there were up to 25,000 people on the waiting list for state-supported housing, and between 3000 and 4,000 new applicants were added to that list each year (Sarr 1984, 10). This far surpassed the estimated 585 houses and 570 plots that the two principal housing agencies – SN-HLM and SICAP – furnished each year (White 1985, 51; ONU Habitat 2012, 2).

The dissatisfaction and concern with state performance in many African societies that the literature points out (Ferguson 2006; Obadare 2009; Bekker and Therborn 2012; Obeng-Odoom 2013; Fredericks 2018; Hoelscher et al. 2023) is very present in Parcelles Assainies. Like in other neighborhoods of Dakar and many cities in the Global South (Chatherjee 2004; 2008; Simone 2004; Cohen 2007; Bob-Milliar and Obeng-Odoom 2011; Anand 2017; Fredericks 2018) people in Parcelles Assainies, since its earliest days, have faced challenges that include insecurity, poor transportation systems, the lack of streetlights, poor sewage and drainage systems, challenges with waste management and limited access to clean water (Sarr 1984; Tall 1994; Ndiaye 2021). During my research in Parcelles Assainies, people often told a sardonic joke about *les Parcelles Assainies qui s'inondent même pendant la saison sèche* (the serviced plots that get flooded even during the dry season). States' failure to deal with these challenges, the political-economic crises of neoliberal economic reforms and struggles over democratization have spawned forms of associational life across African cities that intermittently turn their backs on and actively engage the state (Diop 1992; Simone 2010; Bob-Milliar and Obeng-Odoom 2011; Dimé 2017; Fredericks 2018).

Despite this dissatisfaction with the state in Parcelles Assainies, political trust in the state – the view that the state and its actions are fundamentally benign and that, when it does intervene in communities, it does so in the interest of residents – is high. The biggest complaint with regard to communal welfare often concerns the state's not having carried out enough of its interventions. The desire in these new neighborhoods is to further pull the state in to do more (regularize rights, provide services, etc.) in these communities, not to keep it at bay as people in autochthonous neighborhoods like Cambérène push for.

5.2 Expedited Road Construction in a More Trusting Environment

The greater political trust of residents of Parcelles Assainies in the state enhanced its capacity to construct the VDN 2 in the neighborhood by ensuring local embrace of the project and obviating resistance to it. This dynamic reflects the links between political trust and positive socioeconomic outcomes that have been drawn in the literature (Dearmon and Grier 2009; Faizal et al. 2017; Hutchison and Johnson 2017). People in Parcelles Assainies bought into the broad state narrative about the importance of the project to the emergence of the country with little reserve. Like locals in many other contexts receiving such large-scale infrastructure projects (de Boeck 2011; Harvey and Knox 2015) residents of Parcelles Assainies that live close to the construction site in Unité 15, Unité 9 and Unité 23 that I spoke to invoked many of the potential benefits of the highway. Unlike in Cambérène, however, this appreciation was not clouded by suspicion that the state was building the highway to achieve hidden sinister goals. During my research I did not encounter even one resident of Parcelles Assainies that mentioned or insinuated that the state wanted to build the highway in pursuit of negative hidden schemes. This lack of suspicion extended to the possibility of the state employing a bait-and-switch strategy in the community that states have been accused of in other contexts (Schively 2007, 359). None of the people I interviewed or informally conversed with in the neighborhood expressed concern that once the consent of community members was acquired, the state was going to implement a significantly altered highway design that would harm the neighborhood.

The impact of political trust on the levels of risk that communities hosting infrastructure projects see as acceptable (Schively 2007, 358; Wang et al. 2021) was evident in Parcelles Assainies. Neighborhood residents accepted significantly high levels of risk associated with the highway project. Like in Cambérène, much of the discussion of risks focused on the dangers that a multilane highway posed to those moving between the neighborhood and the beach where neighborhood residents engage in sporting and leisure activities, discard waste, and undertake rituals. Residents of Parcelles Assainies settled on a solution to these challenges with the state that left a significant level of risk uneliminated, falling far short of the zero risk that communities with little trust in project constructors are known to push for (Schively 2007, 358; Holm et al. 2021, 9; Wang et al. 2021). The willingness of the people of Parcelles Assainies to settle on a design with significant risks, unlike their neighbors in Cambérène, indicated their trust that the state would be present after project completion to deal with negative externalities from the project that might materialize. A leader of the Plateform de reverains that advocated on behalf of the community indicated in an interview on July 16, 2018, that they agreed with the state on the posting of signs indicating the speed limit, the installation of speed bumps, and the building of pedestrian bridges over the highway (Interview 24). The project head at AGEROUTE SN partly confirmed this in indicating during a tour of the site in July 2018 that the state would construct three pedestrian bridges over the VDN 2 (Ndiaye F. 2018b).

Posted speed limits, speed bumps, zebra crossings, and pedestrian bridges constituted a solution that left a significant amount of risk for pedestrians. Posted speed limits and speed bumps were going to reduce over speeding on the highway and protect pedestrians from vehicular accidents only when enforced by the police. As traffic across the highway increases, the few pedestrian bridges might encourage people to cross at undesignated points and expose themselves to accidents, requiring the state to build additional bridges in the future. The state would have to repost destroyed signs and maintain speed bumps. The acceptance of this solution demonstrates trust that the state will be there in the future to do this work.

The high political trust in the community was also evident in the timing of efforts to reduce the risks identified for reduction and provide compensation as agreed upon. Because risk reduction measures, such as posting speed limits, building pedestrian bridges, and installing speed bumps, would only be implemented upon the completion of the highway, the agreement attested to the community's trust that the state would carry through on its word and implement the measures agreed upon even after it had completed work on the road. A less trusting community (like Cambérène in this work) would have conditioned allowing work to progress on the highway on either the complete or concomitant reduction of risks.

The tendency of many in the neighborhood to discount the burdens that the project imposed on the community as the unfortunate but, maybe, necessary costs of a beneficial state intervention betrayed the extent to which people in Parcelles Assainies bought into the state narrative on the highway. The unwillingness to resort to aggressive action to compel the state to alleviate these burdens betrayed a willingness in the community to make significant sacrifices and concessions to facilitate what they saw as a state intervention that was positive for the neighborhood, the city, and the country. The state had promised the Plateforme des Riverains de la VDN that the construction site would be regularly watered to reduce dust, that deviation routes would be clearly marked and fitted with speed bumps, and that the work site would be kept well illuminated to ensure security. This was in addition to a slew of compensation promises that, like in Cambérène, included providing jobs for local youth, creating spaces for leisure and sports, improving the drainage and sewage system in the neighborhood, and making pipe-borne water more accessible in the community. But once work commenced, the constructors paid no attention to fulfilling these promises. Of particular concern to many living closest to the construction site was the fact that they did not water the site for long periods, causing a proliferation of respiratory illnesses in the area. They did not always clearly mark or install speed bumps on deviation routes along residential streets, causing accidents (Camara 2018). Their failure to properly install adequate lighting on the construction site led to a spate of robberies and assaults in the area.

In the face of continued inaction by the state, the Plateforme des riverains de la VDN, which led negotiations on behalf of the community, organized marches, issued communiqués, and spoke to the press about the challenges the community faced with the construction process (Agence de Presse Sénégalaise 2018b; Enquête+ 2017). A leader of the Plateforme des riverains told us in an interview on July 16, 2018, that "It is hard to think of one thing that we succeeded in getting them to do" (Interview 24) despite this activism. In spite of this intransigence of the state, people did not opt for aggressive action akin to that seen in Cambérène. They instead tended to cast the nuisance as an unfortunate side effect that was worth enduring in the interest of neighborhood and national progress. Below are the reflections of the platform leader cited above (Interview 24), who was clear about the non-responsiveness of the state.

> This highway is going to be a great asset to the public . . . . I think regardless of what you believe you must admit that the state is constructing a really beautiful structure here. When you look at it against the sea it is just beautiful! Certainly, we knew there will be problems. It has reduced the green spaces and there was a lot of dust and vibrations when they were building it. It was infernal! The windows of some of our houses even cracked due to the vibrations. They didn't always clean the site. Sometimes we were the ones who organized ourselves to clean the place. But in the end, I don't really have a problem with the construction of the road. You know we are talking about the development of a country. Maybe, sometimes we want things to be too easy and that can also be a problem.

Given this absence of aggressive contestation by residents of Parcelles Assainies, construction on the VDN 2 along the neighborhood's coast was smooth and quick. The segment of the road from Parcelles Assainies to the outskirts of Cambérène was completed and opened to traffic in 2018, only a year after the commencement of work. In February 2019, the viaduct connecting the end of the VDN 1 at Nord Foire to the coast of Parcelles Assainies was also opened to traffic, allowing cars to drive on the highway all the way to the edge of Cambérène (Rassoul 2019).

5.3 Autochthony, Trust and Collective action

This opening of the VDN 2 segment in Parcelles Assainies was followed by aggressive local mobilization over the highway that, in many ways, mirrored what had started earlier in Cambérène as the state struggled to get construction going there. This popular revolt in Parcelles Assainies and its timing help clarify the causal mechanisms at work. In line with a large literature that focuses on the importance of the capacity for collective action (Olson 1971; Bates 1981; Tilly 1985; Donaghy 2018), one might hypothesize that even if diverging claims to belonging in the city were causally significant, as argued here, it is through their impact on the capacity for collective action against the state that they influence state capacity for infrastructure development. The argument here would be that claims of autochthony facilitate the capacity for collective action against the state in Cambérène and other autochthonous neighborhoods, and their absence in migrant neighborhoods like Parcelles Assainies saps the ability of people in these neighborhoods to resist the state. The people in Cambérène could resist the state and reshape its plans, while those in Parcelles Assainies just lacked the capacity to do so. This argument coincides with the popular tendency in Dakar to regard Lébou neighborhoods as particularly strong and capable. "Powerful" and "boorish" were the adjectives that an inspector from the state Urban Development Directorate, quoted by Sidibé (2015, 25), used to describe them.

Contrary to this argument, I posit that the dissimilarity between Cambérène and Parcelles Assainies was not one of a difference in the capacity for collective action. It was the fact that low levels of political trust motivated people in Cambérène to confront the state *before and during* road construction, but high levels of political trust in Parcelles Assainies ensured people there decided to violently confront the state only *after* the construction of the highway and the many broken promises that accompanied it.

Despite its repeated promises to the community, the state opened the segment of the VDN 2 along the coast of Parcelles Assainies to traffic without installing the road signs, speed limits, speed bumps, zebra crossings, or pedestrian bridges it had promised. This predictably led to over speeding on the highway and a series of accidents that claimed twelve lives and injured many more over a six-month period in 2019 (Actunet.sn 2019; Ndiaye S. 2019). After condoning broken state promises on alleviating nuisances related to highway construction, the carnage on this segment of the VDN 2 turned out to be the proverbial straw that broke the camel's back, provoking aggressive mobilization by the youth of Parcelles Assainies over the highway.

These confrontations commenced in 2019, at the height of the summer holidays in July, when, as the journalist Thiebou Ndiaye notes, this beautiful stretch of beaches on the outskirts of Dakar "take[s] on the appearance of Copacabana" (Ndiaye T. 2024a). Youths going to and returning from the Parcelles Assainies beach, where many play football and participate in wrestling (*laamb* in Wolof), began to use rocks and car tires to block traffic on the newly constructed VDN 2 highway whenever a car hit someone on the road or when they felt endangered by speeding cars (Ndiaye S. 2019; Sow 2019). These protests were initially spontaneous and unorganized. However, as they gained in frequency, they became more organized as various organizations got involved and tried to claim them. The Plateforme des riverains de la VDN used these protests to re-iterate its long-standing calls for the installation of speed bumps and pedestrian bridges. The mayor of the municipality of Parcelles Assainies, Moussa Sy, in a sign of support for the protests, denounced the accidents and called on the central state authorities involved in the highway construction to make the highway safe for pedestrians (Seneweb News 2019; Sow 2019; Thiam 2019). His office released a communique in early August 2019 threatening to take measures to stop the carnage if the authorities failed to act. Not to be outdone, the Mouvement Parcelles Assainies en marche, led by Moustapha Kane who was seeking to unseat Moussa Sy as mayor of the commune became intimately involved in the protests. They organized press conferences and used social media to sensitize the population and mobilize protesters.[14]

Facing determined youth that frequently rendered the highway unusable and fought running battles with the police, the state adopted the same mix of coercive and conciliatory responses it had employed in Cambérène. It reinforced the complement of security forces quelling these protests to prevent road blockages and re-open roads when they occurred. The highway constructors also hurriedly installed speed bumps on the highway in late August 2019 and quickly built one pedestrian overpass on that segment of the road before the end of 2019 (BuzzSenegal 2019). Two more were constructed over the highway later.

Close observers of politics in Senegal will certainly not be surprised by the capacity for collective action of the residents of Parcelles Assainies. The neighborhood has, over time, gained a reputation as the bane of state leaders who have tried to undermine democratic politics in Senegal. Emblematic of this fearsome reputation is the Y'en a Marre movement, whose main officers are based in Unit 16 of Parcelles Assainies. It is from Parcelles Assainies, where it is "territorially anchored" (Dimé 2022, 67), that a group of rappers and journalists created the movement in 2011 (Dimé 2017, 95). It is from what they often proudly refer to as their "*quartier general*" (headquarters) that they have launched and led campaigns involving mass mobilization by youth, which were central to preventing President Abdoulaye Wade and his successor President Macky Sall from manipulating electoral rules and using violence to prolong their stay in power (Dimé 2017; 2022).

---

[14] See the Facebook post "Luttons contre l'indiscipline au Senegal" of July 27, 2019. www.facebook.com/LuttonsLCIS/posts/2303449086437359 (Accessed May 10, 2024).

A leading instigator of what Dimé has termed a "trans-African dynamic of indocility and dissidence" (Dimé 2022, 57), Y'en a Marre has projected itself from its base in Parcelles Assainies to forge relations with leading activist movements in other African countries. It spearheads a Université Populaire de l'Engagement Citoyen (Popular University of Citizen Engagement) and hosts exiled activists from around the continent in Dakar (Dimé et al. 2021). Y'en a Marre has transformed Parcelles Assainies into a Mecca for activists from around the world, as well as leading foreign state and non-state officials seeking to benefit from the aura of the movement. When the French Minister of Foreign Affairs, Laurent Fabius, visited Senegal in July 2012 to promote the supposed dawn of a new type of relationship between France and its former colonies, it was at their "quartier general" in Parcelles Assainies that Y'en a Marre opted to meet with him (Jeune Afrique 2012).

The lack of aggressive action against the state before and during the construction of the segment of the VDN 2 in Parcelles Assainies was not due to a lack of capacity to undertake collective action by people in the neighborhood. It was the result of a high level of political trust that was betrayed repeatedly by the state during and immediately after the construction exercise, finally forcing the community to adopt aggressive measures after the completion of the highway.

The importance of temporality – when, instead of just whether, events occur – that scholars in the comparative historical tradition emphasize (Pierson 2000; Mahoney 2004; Thelen and Mahoney 2015) comes to the fore here. The historically rooted distrust of the state in Cambérène led to aggressive mobilization to prevent its excesses that people in the neighborhood had come to expect after almost two centuries of interactions marked by what Angrand euphemistically referred to as "multiple difficulties and many incidents" (Angrand 1946, 94). This caused significant delays in the construction of the highway. In Parcelles Assainies, more trusting perceptions of the state led to an embrace of the highway project even when this imposed significant costs on the community, facilitating its quick completion. It took the accumulation of broken promises and abusive conduct by the state and its agents during and after the construction to finally provoke social upheaval in Parcelles Assainies.

6 Conclusion

I argue in this Element that the level of ease with which the Senegalese state was able to construct segments of the VDN 2 highway along the coasts of two neighboring communities in Dakar depended on differences in claims to belonging in the city within these two communities. This explanation is built on an understanding of state capacity to implement development interventions as inherently relational. I show how claims to autochthony in this colonial city have pitted indigenous neighborhoods like Cambérène in age-old struggles around land with the state, leading to deep-seated distrust of the state and a tendency to oppose state interventions in these neighborhoods. This makes it difficult for the state to implement major development interventions in these communities. By contrast, I demonstrate how neighborhoods like Parcelles Assainies, which self-identify as agglomerations of recent migrants in colonial cities like Dakar, lack similar historical struggles over land dispossession with the state, leading to much higher levels of political trust in these communities. This greater trust in the state enhances the ability of the state to carry out development interventions in these neighborhoods by lessening local resistance to these projects.

My argument accords with many scholars of Senegalese politics (Magassouba 1985; Villalón 1995; Mbacké 2005; Diagne 2011; Diagne 2012; Babou 2013; Diouf 2013) in according limited political influence to the religious elites known as marabouts that lead the Sufi orders that most Senegalese belong to (Gueye 2002; Diouf 2013). These religious elites influence many aspects of Senegalese life and enjoy some autonomy in the governance of areas recognized as the capitals of these Sufi orders (Magassouba 1985; Diouf 1992; Villalón 1995; Gueye 2002; Mbacké 2005; Diagne 2011; Babou 2013; Diouf 2013). Because Cambérène is the seat of the Layenne Sufi order (Diagne 2011) while Parcelles Assainies has no such religious significance, one may argue that the marabouts may have instigated local resistance there or dissuaded the state from using repressive methods against the population.

The fact that fierce resistance to the state and the state's response to it through a combination of repression and concessions happened in both neighborhoods undercuts this focus on the unique religious importance of Cambérène. This religious significance of Cambérène does not help us understand why fierce resistance there happened before and during construction, delaying work on the road, but took place only after the completion of the road in Parcelles Assainies. Furthermore, both the composition of those involved in the activism and their methods, which bore an uncanny resemblance to those deployed by other youth movements in Senegal and elsewhere in Africa (Hagberg et al. 2015; Rimondi 2015; Dimé 2017; Ombati 2017) suggest a central role for the youth, instead of the marabouts.

The key contribution of this work to the flourishing literature on African political economy is the link I establish between two proliferating but often separate literatures: one on autochthony and the other on urbanity in Africa. I demonstrate the rewards that bringing these two literatures together in the specific context of colonial cities can offer for our understanding of the capacity of the state to undertake development work. The focus on claims to belonging in the colonial city across neighborhoods, I argue, presents us with one way to unravel and analytically exploit heterogeneity in levels of political trust and state capacity to undertake development interventions. It helps us escape the homogenizing tendency of literatures on state capacity in Africa. The capacity to hold constant the identity of the state, the nature of its intervention (the VDN 2 project), and the general geographical space (the capital city) in which it seeks to undertake its intervention has been critical to demonstrating the effect of different types of neighborhoods on levels of political trust and the capacity of the state to undertake largescale infrastructure projects. This work contributes to the ongoing effort to understand what influences levels of political trust on the continent and its rapidly growing urban landscapes (LeBas 2020; Bob-Milliar and Lauterbach 2021; Resnick and Sivasubramanian 2023).

This argument deploys the fact of being colonial cities as an important scope condition and is built on the understanding that colonial cities in non-settler colonies on the African continent bear certain characteristics that significantly influence their political-economic dynamics. It is, therefore, analytically promising to compare these colonial cities with each other, even when they happen to be located in different countries. One must also be careful in applying lessons from these cities to other urban centers in the countries in which they exist that are not colonial cities. Geographical proximity and existence within the same national political-economic sphere may not necessarily make important dynamics in these urban spheres similar. As Hoelscher et al. (2023) note, urbanity itself does not constitute a sufficient condition for the production and elaboration of certain types of politics. In this Element, I show that digging further into the specific histories of urban centers is analytically useful for making sense of the ability of the state to implement major projects across urban spaces.

While this analysis of states' capacity to implement specific developmental interventions is important, it is also useful, in examining these projects, to reflect on broader questions of social wellbeing, project sustainability, and the contributions of bounded interventions to broader growth and development. What do the politics surrounding the VDN 2 project along the coasts of Cambérène and Parcelles Assainies tell us about development in the city of Dakar and Senegal more broadly? When viewed in this broader light, in which neighborhood – Cambérène or Parcelles Assainies – could one say that there was a "positive outcome"?

The literature on NIMBYism and what is sometimes called "neighborhood defense" sheds some light on this question. States and other opponents of NIMBYism and "neighborhood defenders" are wont to castigate such activism as self-interested crusading that undermines the public good (Gibson 2005, 381;

Schively 2007, 257). It is in this light that many, including Mame Wally, cited at the beginning of Chapter 3, cast activism in Cambérène over the construction of the VDN. The people of Cambérène, it was argued, were emptying the highway of its economic and political promise by forcing motorists to spend an hour on a 500 m stretch of the otherwise completed road. Scholars have also noted the exclusionary bent of some of these movements that seek to keep those cast as "other" out of their neighborhoods (Maney and Abraham 2008; Einstein, Glick, and Palmer 2020; McNee and Pojani 2022).

In line with the literature noting that such activism can sometimes have a positive hue (Einstein, Glick, and Palmer 2020), I would argue for a less condemnatory reading of the aggressive local contestation of the highway project in Cambérène. As scholars have argued concerning similar activism in other contexts (Schively 2007; Harvey 2012), contestation by the residents of Cambérène can be viewed as grassroots organizing that reinforces democracy in Senegal. There is also evidence that, as argued by scholars in other contexts (Woolsink 2000; Schively 2007; Harvey 2012), local activism on the VDN 2 highway in Cambérène went beyond narrow individual and neighborhood concerns. It, for instance tackled broad questions of principle that concern the entire city, including the rights of the people of Dakar to easily and freely access the ocean and the city's beaches. This is a concern that many in the city share as the littoral gets occupied by private developers who sometimes privatize portions of the beach even as frenetic development forces city residents to become ever more dependent on these beaches as spaces of leisure and sports (Sy, Diallo, and Kane 2009; Diallo 2024).

I would argue further that dynamics in Parcelles Assainies and Cambérène reinforce arguments by some scholars (Heiman 1997; McAvoy 1998; Snary 2004) that such activism has sometimes led to improvements in the design of these projects. With hindsight it is clear now that the activism of residents in Cambérène saved users of the beach there from the accidents that continue to affect those crossing the VDN 2 to access the beach in Parcelles Assainies and other neighborhoods. It also led to the construction of a raised highway in Cambérène shown in Figure 5 that makes the beach far easier to reach for those with accessibility challenges than in other neighborhoods. This makes it likely that future contestation over the highway on account of safety and accessibility concerns are less likely to happen in Cambérène than in other neighborhoods along the highway, making the segment of the VDN 2 in Cambérène, more sustainable. If questions of local community welfare and the long-term sustainability of these projects are important, then one has to argue that activism in Cambérène, while "challenging the state" (to use the evocative title of Grindle [1996]) may have been beneficial for the neighborhood, the city and the country alike.

Figure 5 The elevated VDN 2 in Cambérène.

Anarchist and libertarian critiques of top-down technocratic and scientific management of social life (Scott 2012; Hayek 1945) provide another angle from which we can laud the robust contestation of state plans, as it happened in Cambérène. In his reflections on the challenge of a "rational economic order," Hayek notes that "the 'data' required for proper economic policy making and implementation are never for the whole society 'given' to a single mind which could work out the implications, and can never be so given" (1945, 519). It is, therefore, critical for the scientific and technical plans wielded by state officials to be combined with what he refers to the "body of very important but unorganized knowledge ... of the particular circumstances of time and place" that are widely distributed in the community (1945, 521). When states are wont to ignore the views of community members that they often cast as lowly, unsophisticated and narrowly self-interested, confrontational measures by locals, as seen in Cambérène, help ensure the integration of the two types of knowledge to the benefit of local communities and the long-term success and sustainability of state projects alike.

The histories of abusive use of state power that render some communities, like Cambérène, particularly distrustful of the state, constitute a major impediment to the implementation of even very well-meaning and assiduously pursued state projects. The broader pursuit of legitimacy and trust in the eyes of society through policies and practices that are fair and just, and that seek to reverse historical injustices, is critical to the ability of states to pursue a wide set of development interventions. This is because state development interventions, like largescale infrastructure projects, are inextricably enmeshed in wider and historically rooted webs of distributive politics, contestation, and statecraft.

This wider web limits the positive effects of very technical measures like better design, improved accounting and coordination, greater project benefits for local communities, and more participatory approaches proposed by development partners to ensure better development project implementation. This is because these measures do not address the broader, historically rooted relationship between states and various segments of society. These broader attitudes toward the state influence how local communities distinguish between the beneficial and the menacing, and even impact how they comprehend well-meaning efforts by the state to augment benefits for locals in project design and implementation. The widespread local perception of "The wall of shame/ The wall of discord," which the state regarded as an instrument to protect Cambérène from coastal erosion, as an effort to cut the community off from the sea, is a good example.

This Element builds on Peter Ekeh's (1975) highly influential reflections on the impact of colonialism on the relationships between states and societies in Africa. Unlike those who downplay the impact of colonialism on the continent (Hyden 1980; Ayittey 1993; Herbst 2000; Mbembe 2001; Kaplan 2002), Ekeh is one of many scholars (Mamdani 1996; Taiwo 2010; Adebanwi 2017; Idrissa Abdoulaye 2021) that argue that colonialism fundamentally influenced political economic and social dynamics in Africa. Ekeh argues that Africa's colonial experience led to the creation of two publics on the continent- one rooted in primordial ties that Africans relate to in a moral way, and another connected to the modern state that they interact with in an amoral manner (1975). Ekeh's work has inspired a significant body of literature that tends to cast the continent as plagued by state-society tensions as well as inter-group conflicts often focused on ethnicity (Ake 1985; Osaghae 1995; Berman 1998; de Sardan 1999; Igwara 2001; Ukiwo 2005).

One line of criticism of Ekeh's thought has pointed at the significant overlap between the civic and primordial spheres in terms of their modes of operation and citizens' interaction within them (Bayart 1993; Joseph 1997). The perspective here is that Ekeh may have created a stark dichotomy between realms that resemble each other significantly and that he may have used too convivial, placid, and moral a brush to paint primordial publics on the continent (Ukiwo 2005; Onoma 2018). While critical, this argument does not problematize the portrayal of the civic public as one to which Africans relate in an undifferentiated manner with an amoral compass.

In this work, I approach Ekeh's (1975) thesis from another angle, going beyond the homogenization of Africans' attitudes toward the civic public. With a focus on colonial cities, I argue that African communities have not experienced the colonial state and its postcolonial successor in the same way and that these differences in their experiences affect how they relate to the state and the success with which the state engages with and intervenes in society. Ekeh (1975) may have proffered an image of the civic public that lacks the nuance necessary to make sense of the diverse ways in which Africans have encountered the state and how this has shaped their perceptions of it. While focusing on historically rooted causes, I show how the continued abuse of rights by postcolonial states (what Ndlovu-Gatsheni [2013] refers to as the "coloniality" of the postcolonial state) and the refusal of these states to reverse colonial ills are hampering even well-intentioned state efforts at development interventions.

Abbreviations

Ageroute SN	Agence des Travaux et de Gestion des Routes au Sénégal
ANSD	Agence nationale de la statistique et de la démographie
BAHSO	Bureau d'assistance aux collectivités pour l'habitat social
BHS	Banque de l'Habitat du Sénégal
BRT	Bus Rapid Transit
HAMO	Société des habitations modernes
HIV/AIDS	Human Immunodeficiency Virus/Acquired Immuno deficiency Syndrome
NIMBY	Not in my backyard
OHLM	Office des habitations à loyer modéré
PIDA	Program for Infrastructure Development in Africa
SCAT-URBAM	Société centrale d'aménagement des terrains urbains
SICAP	Société immobilière du Cap-Vert
SN-HLM	Société nationale des habitations à loyer modéré
TER	Train Express Régional
VDN	Voie de dégagement nord

References

Actunet.sn., 2019. "Alerte – La Vdn Tue 12 Personnes en 6 Mois." Adakar.com, August 6. http://news.adakar.com/h/111111.html (Accessed May 6, 2024).

Adebanwi, W., 2017. Africa's "two publics": Colonialism and governmentality. *Theory, Culture & Society*, *34*(4), pp.65–87.

Adesina, J., 2021. Social policy in the African context: An introduction. In Adesina, J. ed. *Social policy in the African context*, pp.1–12. CODESRIA.

Adunbi, O., 2019. (Re) inventing development: China, infrastructure, sustainability and special economic zones in Nigeria. *Africa*, *89*(4), pp.662–679.

Agbiboa, D. E., 2020. How informal transport systems drive African cities. *Current History*, *119*(817), pp.175–181.

Agence de Presse Sénégalaise, 2018a. "Sénégal: Délocalisation de l'émissaire de Cambérène – Le CIDEC veut le 'respect des engagements dans les meilleurs délais'." Allafrica.com. August 21. https://fr.allafrica.com/stories/201808210608.html (Accessed May 3, 2018).

Agence de Presse Sénégalaise, 2018b. "Sénégal: Les riverains de la VDN présentent leur mémorandum, Dimanche." Allafrica.com, June 20. https://fr.allafrica.com/stories/201806210320.html (Accessed May 6, 2024).

Agence de Presse Sénégalaise, 2020. "Sénégal: Discours du chef de l'Etat à la Nation à l'occasion du nouvel an." December 31. https://fr.allafrica.com/stories/202101020004.html.

Ake, C., 1985. *Political economy of Nigeria*. Longman.

Akpan, U., 2014. Impact of regional road infrastructure improvement on intra-regional trade in ECOWAS. *African Development Review*, *26*(S1), pp.64–76.

Allina-Pisano, J., 2009. How to tell an axe murderer: An essay on ethnography, truth, and lies. In Schatz, E. ed. *Political ethnography: What immersion contributes to the study of power* (pp.53–73). University of Chicago Press.

Alves, A. C., 2013. China's "win-win" cooperation: Unpacking the impact of infrastructure-for-resources deals in Africa. *South African Journal of International Affairs*, *20*(2), pp.207–226.

Amsden, A. H., 1989. *Asia's next giant: South Korea and late industrialization*. Oxford University Press.

Anand, N., 2017. *Hydraulic city: Water and the infrastructures of citizenship in Mumbai*. Duke University Press.

Angrand, A. P., 1946. *Les Lébous de la Presqu'ile Du Cap-Vert: Essai Sur Leur Histoire Et Leurs Coutumes*. E. Gensul.

References

ANSD (Agence Nationale De La Statistique et de la Demographie), 2016. "La Population du Sénégal en 2016: Un Extrait des Projections Démographiques du RGPHAE 2013." (December).

Antoine, P. and Savané, L., 1990. Urbanisation et migration en Afrique. In *Union for African population studies (dir.), conference on the role of migration in Africa development issues and policies for the 90s: Dakar, Union for African Population Studies* (pp.55–81). Union for African Population Studies.

Appel, H., Anand, N., and Gupta, A., 2018. Temporality, politics, and the promise of infrastructure. In Anand, N., Gupta, A., and Appel, H., eds. *The Promise of Infrastructure* (pp. 1–38). Duke University Press.

Archer, D. N., 2020. "White Men's Roads through Black Men's Homes": Advancing racial equity through highway reconstruction. *Vanderbilt Law Review*, 73, p.1259.

Asongu, S. A. and Aminkeng, G. A., 2013. The economic consequences of China – Africa relations: Debunking myths in the debate. *Journal of Chinese Economic and Business Studies*, 11(4), pp.261–277.

Ayittey, G. B. N., 1993. *Africa betrayed*. St Martin's Press.

Babou, C. A., 2013. The Senegalese "social contract" revisited: The Muridiyya Muslim Order and state politics in postcolonial Senegal. In Diouf. M. ed. *Tolerance, democracy, and sufis in Senegal* (pp.125–146). Columbia University Press.

Balaton-Chrimes, S., 2013. Indigeneity and Kenya's Nubians: Seeking equality in difference or sameness? *The Journal of Modern African Studies*, 51(2), pp.331–354.

Bates, R. H., 1981. *Markets and states in tropical Africa: The political basis of agricultural policies*. University of California Press.

Bates, R. H., 1993. "Urban bias": A fresh look. *The Journal of Development Studies*, 29(4), pp.219–228.

Bayart, J. F., 1993. *The state in Africa: The politics of the belly*. Addison-Wesley Longman.

Bayart, J. F., Ellis, S., and Hibou, B., 1999. *The criminalization of the state in Africa*. Indiana University Press.

Beckman, B., 1991. Empowerment or repression? The World Bank and the politics of African adjustment. *Africa Development/Afrique et Développement*, 16(1), pp.45–72.

Bekker, S. B. and Therborn, G., 2012. Introduction. In Bekker, S. B. and Therborn, G. eds. *Capital cities in Africa: Power and powerlessness* (pp. 1–6). HSRC Press.

References

Benton, A., 2015. *HIV exceptionalism: Development through disease in Sierra Leone*. University of Minnesota Press.

Berman, B. J., 1998. Ethnicity, patronage and the African state: The politics of uncivil nationalism. *African Affairs*, 97(388), pp.305–341.

Berry, S., 2000. *Chiefs know their boundaries: Essays on property, power, and the past in Asante, 1896–1996*. Heinemann.

Berry, S., 2002. Debating the land question in Africa. *Comparative Studies in Society and History*, 44(4), pp.638–668.

Bob-Milliar, G., 2014. Party youth activists and low-intensity electoral violence in Ghana: A qualitative study of party foot soldiers' activism. *African Studies Quarterly*, 15(1), pp.125–152.

Bob-Milliar, G. M. and Lauterbach, K., 2021. The generation of trust in political parties in Ghana. *Africa Today*, 68(2), pp.81–98.

Bob-Milliar, G. M. and Obeng-Odoom, F., 2011. The informal economy is an employer, a nuisance, and a goldmine: Multiple representations of and responses to informality in Accra, Ghana. *Urban Anthropology and Studies of Cultural Systems and World Economic Development*, 40 (3/4), pp.263–284.

Bocoum, M., 2013. "Abdoulaye Makhtar Diop Sera-T-Il L'homme Du Consensus?: Succession Des Deux Grands Serigne De Dakar." SenePlus, March 28. www.seneplus.com/article/abdoulaye-makhtar-diop-sera-t-il-lhomme-du-consensus (Accessed May 3, 2024).

Bocquier, P., 2004. "Analyzing urbanization in sub-Saharan Africa." In Champion, T. and Hugo, G., eds. *New forms of urbanization: Beyond the urban-rural dichotomy* (pp. 133–150). Ashgate Publishing.

Boeck, F. D., 2011. Inhabiting ocular ground: Kinshasa's future in the light of Congo's spectral urban politics. *Cultural Anthropology*, 26(2), pp.263–286.

Bonhoure, L., 2015. "Les Dessous D'une Révolte: Contestation Des Jeunes De Ngor, Ouakam Et Yoff," SenePlus, May 20. www.seneplus.com/article/les-dessous-d'une-révolte (Accessed May 3, 2024).

Boone, C., 2003. *Political topographies of the African state: Territorial authority and institutional choice*. Cambridge University Press.

Boone, C., 2017. Sons of the soil conflict in Africa: Institutional determinants of ethnic conflict over land. *World Development*, 96, pp.276–293.

Bouchard, G., 2013. National myths: An overview. In Bouchard, G., ed. *National myths: Constructed pasts, contested presents* (pp.276–289). Routledge.

Bouche, D., 1978. Dakar pendant la deuxième Guerre mondiale: Problèmes de surpeuplement. *Outre-Mers: Revue d'histoire*, 65(240), pp.423–438.

Branch, A. and Mampilly, Z., 2015. *Africa uprising: Popular protest and political change*. Bloomsbury.

Bratton, M., 1994. Peasant-state relations in postcolonial Africa: Patterns of engagement and disengagement. In Migdal, J., Kohli, A., and Shue, V. eds. *State power and social forces: Domination and transformation in the third world* (pp.231–254). Cambridge University Press.

Bratton, M. and Gyimah-Boadi, E., 2016. Do trustworthy institutions matter for development? Corruption, trust, and government performance in Africa. *Afrobarometer Dispatch*, August 23 (112), p.6.

Buzz Senegal, 2019. "Prolongement de la VDN: Les Passerelles Seront Posées d'ici le 24 Septembre," Sene360.sn, September 4. www.buzzsenegal.com/news/News/prolongement-de-la-vdn-les-passerelles-s_n_40896.html (Accessed May 6, 2024).

Byerlee, D., 1974. Rural-urban migration in Africa: Theory, policy and research implications. *International Migration Review*, 8(4), pp.543–566.

Calderon, C. A. and Serven, L., 2014. The effects of infrastructure development on growth and income distribution. *Annals of Economics and Finance*, 15(2), pp.521–534.

Callaghy, T. M., 1987. The state as lame leviathan: The patrimonial administrative state in Africa. In Ergas Z. ed. *The African state in transition* (pp.87–116). Palgrave Macmillan UK.

Callaghy, T. M. and Ravenhill, J., 1993. How hemmed in? Lessons and prospects of Africa's responses to decline. In Callaghy, T. M. and Ravenhill, J., eds. *Hemmed in: Responses to Africa's economic decline* (pp.520–563). Columbia University Press.

Calvet, M. J. and Ragon, C. J. 1982. "Histoire de Dakar: Documents Publié par le Service Culturel de l'Ambassade de France au Sénégal Lors de la Visite du Président Français en 1982," Unpublished document accessed in the Archives Nationales du Sénégal.

Camara, M., 2018. "Prolongement De La VDN: Désagrément, Poussière, Quand Une Solution Crée De Nouveaux Problems," Senenews.com. March 6. www.senenews.com/actualites/prolongement-de-la-vdn-desagrement-poussiere-quand-une-solution-cree-de-nouveaux-problemes_222660.html (Accessed May 6, 2024).

Camara, A. and de Benoist, J. R. D. 2003. *Histoire de Gorée*. Maisonneuve and Larosse.

Cammett, M. and Maclean, L. M., 2014. Introduction. In Cammett, M. and Maclean, L. M., eds. *The politics of non-state social welfare* (pp.1–16). Cornell University Press.

Chabal, P. and Daloz, J. P., 1999. *Africa works: Disorder as political instrument*. Indiana University Press.

References

Chatterjee, P., 2004. *The politics of the governed: Reflections on popular politics in most of the world.* Columbia University Press.

Chatterjee, P., 2008. India's divide: Economic growth and marginalized groups. *The Brown Journal of World Affairs, 14*(2), pp.139–147.

Chiyemura, F., Gambino, E., and Zajontz, T., 2023. Infrastructure and the politics of African state agency: Shaping the belt and road initiative in East Africa. *Chinese Political Science Review, 8*(1), pp.105–131.

Citrin, J. and Stoker, L., 2018. Political trust in a cynical age. *Annual Review of Political Science, 21*(1), pp.49–70.

Cohen, M., 2007. Aid, density, and urban form: Anticipating Dakar. *Built Environment, 33*(2), pp.145–156.

Commune de Parcelles Assainies, 2016. "Guide Municipal Année 2016."

Commune de Parcelles Assainies, 2018. "Guide Municipal Année 2018: Vivre la ville ensemble."

Coquery-Vidrovitch, C., 1972. *Le Congo au temps des grandes compagnies concessionnaires 1898–1930.* Éditions de l'École des hautes études en sciences sociales.

Coquery-Vidrovitch, C., 1991. The process of urbanization in Africa (from the origins to the beginning of independence). *African Studies Review, 34*(1), pp.1–98.

Coquery-Vidrovitch, C., 1993. *Histoire des villes d'Afrique noire.* Albin Michel.

Currie, I. P., Otero-Bahamon, S., and Uribe, S., 2021. What is the state made of? Coca, roads, and the materiality of state formation in the frontier. *World Development, 141,* p.105395.

DakarActu, 2018. "Prolongement de la VDN Section 2: La Fin des Travaux Prévue en Décembre Prochain," *Dakaractu,* July 4. www.dakaractu.com/PROLONGEMENT-DE-LA-VDN-SECTION-2-La-fin-des-travaux-prevue-en-decembre-prochain_a154316.html (Accessed May 3, 2024).

Daland, R. T., 1981. *Exploring Brazilian bureaucracy: Performance and pathology.* University Press of America.

De Benoist, J. R., 2008. *Histoire de l'Église catholique au Sénégal: du milieu du XVe siècle à l'aube du troisième millénaire.* Karthala Editions.

De Sardan, J. O., 1999. A moral economy of corruption in Africa? *The Journal of Modern african Studies, 37*(1), pp.25–52.

Dear, M., 1992. Understanding and overcoming the NIMBY syndrome. *Journal of the American Planning Association, 58*(3), pp.288–300.

Dearmon, J. and Grier, K., 2009. Trust and development. *Journal of Economic Behavior & Organization, 71*(2), pp.210–220.

Di Nunzio, M., 2018. Anthropology of infrastructure. *LSE Cities, Governing Infrastructure Interfaces-Research Note*, *1*, pp.1–4.

Di Nunzio, M., 2022. Evictions for development: Creative destruction, redistribution and the politics of unequal entitlements in inner-city Addis Ababa (Ethiopia), 2010–2018. *Political Geography*, *98*, p.102671.

Diagne, M., 2011. *Pouvoir politique et espaces religieux au Sénégal: la gouvernance locale à Touba, Cambérène et Médina Baye* (Doctoral dissertation, Université du Québec à Montréal).

Diagne, M., 2012. La Réapparition du Patrimoine Cultuel par les Jeunes Layennes de Cambérène: Fondements et Actions des Associations Communautaires. In Gomez-Perz, M. and Leblanc, N. eds. *L'Afrique des Générations: Entre Tension et Négociations* (pp. 165–215). Karthala.

Diagne, M., 2020. "Finalement, Ils Ont Fait Pire Que Les Wade Avec Nos Terres," SenePlus, June 8. www.seneplus.com/opinions/finalement-ils-ont-fait-pire-que-les-wade-avec-nos-terres (Accessed May 3, 2024).

Diagne, S. B., 2004. On prospective: Development and a political culture of time. *Africa Development*, *29*(1), pp.55–69.

Diallo, I., 2016. "La Révolte Des Lébous Contre Le 'Bradage' Du Foncier Autour De L'aéroport De Dakar," Le360Afrique.com, April 28. http://afrique.le360.ma/senegal/societe/2016/04/28/2020-la-revolte-des-lebous-contre-le-bradage-du-foncier-autour-de-laeroport-de-dakar-2020 (Accessed May 3, 2024).

Diallo, I., 2024. "Le rapport qui accable les prédateurs du littoral dakarois," Seneplus. August 14. www.seneplus.com/societe/un-rapport-pointant-des-irregularites-preoccupantes-entre-les (Accessed February 18, 2025).

Diamond, J., 1999. *Guns, germs and steel: The fates of human societies*. W.W. Norton.

Dieng, D., 2018. "Macky Sall Abdique Devant les Populations de Camberene," *Seneplus*, July 4. www.seneplus.com/societe/macky-sall-abdique-devant-les-populations-de-camberene (Accessed May 3, 2024).

Dijkstra, A. G. and Van Donge, J. K., 2001. What does the 'show case' show? Evidence of and lessons from adjustment in Uganda. *World Development*, *29*(5), pp.841–863.

Dill, B., 2013. *Fixing the African state: Recognition, politics, and community-based development in Tanzania* (pp.119–147). Palgrave Macmillan US.

Dimé, M., 2017. De bul faale à Y'en a marre: continuités et dissonances dans les dynamiques de contestation sociopolitique et d'affirmation citoyenne chez les jeunes au Sénégal. *Africa Development*, *42*(2), pp.83–105.

Dimé, M., 2022. Y'en a Marre: Catalyst for an indocility grammar in Senegal. In Sanches, E. R. ed. *Popular protest, political opportunities, and change in Africa* (pp.56–72). Routledge.

Dimé, M., Kapagama, P., Soré, Z., and Touré, I., 2021. Afrikki mwinda. *Africa Development*, *46*(1), pp.71–92.

Diop, A., 2012. Dakar. In Bekker, S. B. and Therborn, G. eds. *Capital cities in Africa: Power and powerlessness* (pp.32–45). HSRC Press.

Diop, M. C., 1992. Du "Socialism" au "Liberalism": Les Legitimites de l'Etat. In Diop, M. C. ed. *Senegal: Trajectoires d'un etat* (pp.13–38). CODESRIA.

Diop, P. M., 1993. "Contribution a l'Etude du Changement Social Chez les Lébous de la Presqu'ile du Cap Vert" (Master's Thesis, Université Cheikh Anta Diop).

Diouf, M., 1990. *Le Kajoor au XIXe siècle: pouvoir ceddo et conquête coloniale*. Karthala Editions.

Diouf, M., 1992. Le Clientelism, la "Technocratie" et Apres? In Diop, M. C. ed. *Senegal: Trajectoires d'un Etat* (pp.233–278). CODESRIA.

Diouf, M., 2013. Introduction: The public role of the "good Islam": Sufi Islam and the administration of pluralism. In Diouf, M. ed. *Tolerance, Democracy, and Sufis in Senegal* (pp.1–35). Columbia University Press.

Donaghy, M. M., 2018. *Democratizing urban development: Community organizations for housing across the United States and Brazil*. Temple University Press.

Doner, R. F. and Schneider, B. R., 2000. Business associations and economic development: Why some associations contribute more than others. *Business and Politics*, *2*(3), pp.261–288.

Easton, D., 1975. A re-assessment of the concept of political support. *British Journal of Political Science*, *5*(4), pp.435–457.

Echenberg, M., 2002. Black death, white medicine: Bubonic plague and the politics of public health in colonial Senegal, 1914–1945. Heinemann.

Einstein, K. L., Glick, D. M., and Palmer, M., 2020. Neighborhood defenders: Participatory politics and America's housing crisis. *Political Science Quarterly*, *135*(2), pp.281–312.

Ekeh, P. P., 1975. Colonialism and the two publics in Africa: A theoretical statement. *Comparative Studies in Society and History*, *17*(1), pp.91–112.

Elfversson, E. and Höglund, K., 2018. Home of last resort: Urban land conflict and the Nubians in Kibera, Kenya. *Urban Studies*, *55*(8), pp.1749–1765.

Emedia, 2020. "L'intégralité du discours de Macky Sall," SenePlus, December 31. www.seneplus.com/politique/lintegralite-du-discours-de-macky-sall (Accessed May 6, 2024).

Enquete+, 2017. "Travaux 2e section de dégagement Nord (Vdn): Inquiétudes des riverains, assurances de l'Ageroute," aDakar.com, October 3. http://news.adakar.com/h/91044.html (Accessed May 6, 2024).

Enriquez, E., Sybblis, M., and Centeno, M. A., 2017. A cross-national comparison of sub-national variation. *American Behavioral Scientist*, *61*(8), pp.908–931.

Evans, P. B., 1995. *Embedded autonomy: States and industrial transformation*. Princeton University Press.

Faizal, S. M., Palil, M. R., Maelah, R., and Ramli, R., 2017. Perception on justice, trust and tax compliance behavior in Malaysia. *Kasetsart Journal of Social Sciences*, *38*(3), pp.226–232.

Fal, I., 2015. "Macky Et Le Bradage Du Littoral," SenePlus, February 1. www.seneplus.com/article/macky-et-le-bradage-du-littoral (Accessed May 3, 2024).

Fall, A. S. F., 1995. Relations à Distance des Migrants et Réseaux d'Insertion à Dakar. In Antoine, P. and Diop, A. B. eds., *La Ville a Guichet Fermé? Itinéraires, Reseaux et Insertion Urbain* (pp.257–275). IFAN/ORSTOM.

Fallers, L. A., 1961. Are African cultivators to be called "peasants"? *Current Anthropology*, *2*(2), pp.108–110.

Faure, C., 1914. *Histoire de presqu'île du Cap Vert et des origines de Dakar*. É. Larose.

Favilukis, J., Mabille, P., and Van Nieuwerburgh, S., 2023. Affordable housing and city welfare. *The Review of Economic Studies*, *90*(1), pp.293–330.

Faye, C., 2015. "Accaparement des terres, réformes foncières, expropriation: La 'bombe' foncière risque de détonner au Sénégal," Sud Online, July 6. www.farmlandgrab.org/post/view/25105-la-bombe-fonciere-risque-de-detonner-au-senegal (Accessed May 3, 2024).

Faye, I. M., Benkahla, A., Touré, O., Seck, S. M., and Ba, C. O., 2011. *Les acquisitions de terres à grande échelle au Sénégal: description d'un nouveau phénomène*, Dakar, Initiative prospective agricole et rurale. IPAR.

Feigenbaum, H., Henig, J., and Hamnett, C., 1998. *Shrinking the state: The political underpinnings of privatization*. Cambridge University Press.

Ferguson, J., 2006. *Global shadows: Africa in the neoliberal world order*. Duke University Press.

Ferrante, L., Andrade, M. B., and Fearnside, P. M., 2021. Land grabbing on Brazil's Highway BR-319 as a spearhead for Amazonian deforestation. *Land Use Policy*, *108*, p.105559.

Foster, D. and Warren, J., 2022. The NIMBY problem. *Journal of Theoretical Politics*, *34*(1), pp.145–172.

Fotsch, P. M., 2007. *Watching the traffic go by: Transportation and isolation in urban America*. University of Texas Press.

Fourchard, L., 2009. Dealing with "strangers": Allocating urban space to migrants in Nigeria and french west Africa, end of the nineteenth century to 1960. In Locatelli, F. and Nugent, P. eds. *African Cities* (pp.187–217). Brill.

Fredericks, R., 2018. *Garbage citizenship: Vital infrastructures of labor in Dakar, Senegal*. Duke University Press.

Freund, B., 2007. *The African city: A history* (Vol. 4). Cambridge University Press.

Fujii, L. A., 2010. Shades of truth and lies: Interpreting testimonies of war and violence. *Journal of Peace Research*, 47(2), pp.231–241.

Fujii, L. A., 2017. *Interviewing in social science research: A relational approach*. Routledge.

Gary, I., 1996. Confrontation, co-operation or co-optation: NGOs and the Ghanaian state during structural adjustment. *Review of African Political Economy*, 23(68), pp.149–168.

Gaye, M., 2018. "Destruction du mur de Camberène: Face à la pression des Layènes, Macky recule," Walf Group, July 4. https://walf-groupe.com/blog/2018/07/04/destruction-mur-de-camberene-face-a-pression-layenes-macky-recule/ (Accessed May 3, 2024).

Geda, A. and Seid, E. H., 2015. The potential for internal trade and regional integration in Africa. *Journal of African Trade*, 2(1), pp.19–50.

Geschiere, P., 2009. *The perils of belonging: Autochthony, citizenship, and exclusion in Africa and Europe*. University of Chicago Press.

Geschiere, P. and Nyamnjoh, F. B., 2000. Capitalism and autochthony: The seesaw of mobility and belonging. *Public Culture*, 12(2), pp.423–452.

Gibson, T. A., 2005. NIMBY and the civic good. *City & Community*, 4(4), pp.381–401.

Goerg, O., 1989. Chefs de Quartier et "Tribal Headman": Deux visions des Colonisés en Ville. In Chretien, J.-P. and Prunier, G. eds. *Les ethnies ont une histoire* (pp.269–270). KARTHALA.

Goerg, O., 1990. La genèse du peuplement de Conakry. *Cahiers d'études africaines*, 30(117), pp.73–99.

Goerg, O., 1993. La Guinée Conakry. In Soulillou, J. ed. *Rives Coloniales: Architectures de Saint-Louis a Doula* (pp.79–104). Editions Parenthèses/ Editions de l'Orstom.

Goerg, O., 1998. From Hill Station (Freetown) to Downtown Conakry (First Ward): Comparing French and British approaches to segregation in colonial cities at the beginning of the twentieth century. *Canadian Journal of African Studies*, 32(1), pp.1–31.

Goerg, O., 2006. Chieftainships between past and present: From city to suburb and back in colonial Conakry, 1890s–1950s. *Africa Today*, 52(4), pp.3–27.

Goerg, O., 2012. "Conakry." In Bekker, S. B. and Therborn, G., eds. *Capital Cities in Africa: Power and Powerlessness* (pp. 8–31). HSRC Press.

Gough, I. and Wood, G., 2004. *Insecurity and welfare regimes in Asia, Africa and Latin America: Social policy in development contexts.* Cambridge University Press.

Gouws, A. and Schulz-Herzenberg, C., 2016. What's trust got to do with it? Measuring levels of political trust in South Africa 20 years after democratic transition. *Politikon, 43*(1), pp.7–29.

Grindle, M. S., 1996. *Challenging the state: Crisis and innovation in Latin America and Africa.* Cambridge University Press.

Grindle, M. S., 1997. Divergent cultures? When public organizations perform well in developing countries. *World Development, 25*(4), pp.481–495.

Grindle, M. S., 2004. *Despite the odds: The contentious politics of education reform.* Princeton University Press.

Grindle, M. S. and Thomas, J. W., 1991. *Public choices and policy change.* Johns Hopkins University Press.

Guèye, C., 2002. *Touba: la capitale des mourides.* Karthala Editions.

Gueye, M. M., 2013. "Pourquoi Y A-T-Il Toujours Deux « Serigne Ndakaru »?" Dakaractu, February 7. www.dakaractu.com/POURQUOI-Y-A-T-IL-TOUJOURS-DEUX-SERIGNE-NDAKARU_a38633.html (Accessed May 3, 2024).

Gueye, M. R., 2020. "Aéroport Léopold Sédar Senghor: Le Cheanacs dénonce le dépeçage de 557 parcelles par des pontes de la République," Seneweb.com, September 30. www.seneweb.com/news/Societe/aeroport-leopold-sedar-senghor-le-cheana_n_329996.html (Accessed May 3, 2024).

Hagberg, S., Kibora, L., and Ouattara, F. et al., 2015. Au cœur de la révolution burkinabè. *Anthropologie & développement,* 42–42(42–43), pp.199–224.

Haggard, S., 2018. *Developmental states.* Cambridge University Press.

Halisi, C. R. D., Kaiser, P. J., and Ndegwa, S. N., 1998. Guest editors' introduction: The multiple meanings of citizenship: rights, identity, and social justice in Africa. *Africa Today, 45*(3/4), pp.337–349.

Handzic, K., 2010. Is legalized land tenure necessary in slum upgrading? Learning from Rio's land tenure policies in the Favela Bairro Program. *Habitat International, 34*(1), pp.11–17.

Harvey, D., 2003. *The new imperialism.* Oxford University Press. https://doi.org/10.1093/oso/9780199264315.001.0001.

Harvey, D., 2012. *Rebel cities: From the right to the city to the urban revolution.* Verso books.

Harvey, P. and Knox, H., 2015. *Roads: An anthropology of infrastructure and expertise.* Cornell University Press.

Hayek, F. A., 1945. The use of knowledge in society. *The American Economic Review, 35*(4), pp.519–530.

Heiman, M. K., 1997. Science by the people: Grassroots environmental monitoring and the debate over scientific expertise. *Journal of Planning Education and Research*, *16*(4), pp.291–299.

Herbst, J., 2000. *States and power in Africa: Comparative lessons in authority and control*. Princeton University Press.

Heredia, B. and Schneider, B. R., 2003. The political economy of administrative reform in developing countries. In Schneider, B. R. and Heredia, B. eds., *Reinventing leviathan: The politics of administrative reform in developing countries* (pp.1–29). North-South Center Press, University of Miami.

Hetherington, M. J., 1998. The political relevance of political trust. *American Political Science Review*, *92*(4), pp.791–808.

Hoelscher, K., Dorward, N., Fox, S., et al., 2023. Urbanization and political change in Africa. *African Affairs*, *122*(488), pp.353–376.

Holland, A. C., 2023. Roadblocks: How property rights undermine development in Colombia. *American Journal of Political Science*, *67*(3), pp.639–655.

Hollands, G., 2007. *Corruption in infrastructure delivery: South Africa*. Loughborough University.

Holm, R. H., Chunga, B. A., Mallory, A., Hutchings, P., and Parker, A., 2021. A qualitative study of NIMBYism for waste in smaller urban areas of a low-income country, Mzuzu, Malawi. *Environmental Health Insights*, *15*, p.11786302209841 47.

Honwana, A. M., 2012. *The time of youth: Work, social change, and politics in Africa*. Lynne Rienner.

Hull, R., 1976. *African cities and towns before the European conquest*. W.W. Norton.

Hutchison, M. L. and Johnson, K., 2011. Capacity to trust? Institutional capacity, conflict, and political trust in Africa, 2000–2005. *Journal of Peace Research*, *48*(6), pp.737–752.

Hur, A., 2022. *Narratives of civic duty: How national stories shape democracy in Asia*. Cornell University Press.

Hyden, G., 1980. *Beyond Ujamaa in Tanzania: Underdevelopment and an uncaptured peasantry*. University of California Press.

Hyden, G., 2008. The economy of affection: Why the African peasantry remains uncaptured. In *Contemporary perspectives on African moral economy* (pp.16–32).

Idrissa Abdoulaye, A., 2021. The Sahel: A cognitive mapping. *New Left Review*, 132 (Nov/Dec), pp.5–39.

Igwara, O., 2001. Dominance and difference: Rival visions of ethnicity in Nigeria. *Ethnic and Racial Studies*, *24*(1), pp.86–103.

Jackson, R. H., 1990. *Quasi-states: Sovereignty, international relations and the third world* (Vol. 12). Cambridge University Press.

Jackson, S., 2006. Sons of which soil? The language and politics of autochthony in Eastern DR Congo. *African Studies Review*, *49*(2), pp.95–124.

Jedwab, R. and Storeygard, A., 2019. Economic and political factors in infrastructure investment: Evidence from railroads and roads in Africa 1960–2015. *Economic History of Developing Regions*, *34*(2), pp.156–208.

Jeune Afrique, 2012. "Sénégal: Laurent Fabius salue 'l'exemple' du mouvement 'Y'en a marre'," July 28. www.jeuneafrique.com/151758/politique/s-n-gal-laurent-fabius-salue-l-exemple-du-mouvement-y-en-a-marre/ (accessed October 7, 2024).

Johnston, R. J., 1991. A question of place: Exploring the practice of human geography. In *A question of place: Exploring the practice of human geography*. Blackwell.

Joseph, R., 1997. Democratization in Africa after 1989: Comparative and theoretical perspectives. *Comparative Politics*, *29*(3), pp.363–382.

Joseph, R., 2003. Africa: States in crisis. *Journal of Democracy*, *14*, p.159.

Jost, G., 1968. L'urbanisme et l'aspect de la ville. In Sankale, M., Thomas, L. V., and Fougeyrollas, P. eds. *Dakar en devenir* (pp.49–78). Presence Africaine.

Kaplan, R. D., 2002. *The coming anarchy: Shattering the dreams of the post cold war*. Vintage.

Kaufman, R., 2003. The comparative politics of administrative reform: Some implications for theory and practice. In Schnieder, B. R. and Heredia, B. eds. *Reinventing Leviathan: The politics of administrative reform in developing countries* (pp.281–302). North-South Center Press, University of Miami.

Khouma, M., 2007. Anticipation de la ville et production de l'espace dans la couronne périurbaine de Dakar. In Piermay, J-L. and Sarr, C., eds. *La ville sénégalaise une invention aux frontières du monde* (pp.57–74). Karthala.

Kiennemann, L., 2023. "Sénégal: construire une gendarmerie ou un lycée? Un litige foncier enflamme une commune de Dakar," France24, May 12. https://observers.france24.com/fr/afrique/20230512-sénégal-dakar-ngor-affrontements-violents-population-gendarmerie-litige-foncier (Accessed May 3, 2024).

King, A. D., 1985. Colonial cities: Global pivots of change. In *Colonial cities: Essays on urbanism in a colonial context* (pp.7–32). Martinus Nijhoff Publishers.

Kohli, A., 2004. *State-directed development: Political power and industrialization in the global periphery*. Cambridge University Press.

Konings, P., 2008. Autochthony and ethnic cleansing in the post-colony: The 1966 Tombel disturbances in Cameroon. *The International Journal of African Historical Studies*, *41*(2), pp.203–222.

Kushner, D. C. and MacLean, L. M., 2015. Introduction to the special issue: The politics of the nonstate provision of public goods in Africa. *Africa Today*, 62(1), pp. vii–xvii.

Kwak, N. H., 2018. Slum clearance as a transnational process in globalizing Manila. In Sandoval-Strausz, A. K. and Kwak, N. eds. *Making cities global: The transnational turn in urban history* (pp.98–113). University of Pennsylvania Press.

La Fontaine, J. S., 1970. *City politics: A study of Leopoldville, 1962–63*. Cambridge University Press.

Landau, L. 2012. "Introducing the demons." Exorcising the Demons Within: Xenophobia, Violence and Statecraft in Contemporary South Africa (pp.1–25). United Nations University Press.

Landell-Mills, P., Agarwala, R., and Please, S., 1989. Sub-Saharan Africa: From crisis to sustainable growth: A long-term perspective study. World Ban.

Le Quotidien., 2018. "CAMBERENE – Tensions autour du prolongement de la Vdn: Les pêcheurs interpellent le Président Macky Sall," Le Quotidien. March 1. https://lequotidien.sn/camberene-tensions-autour-du-prolongement-de-la-vdn-les-pecheurs-interpellent-le-president-macky-sall/ (Accessed May 3, 2024).

Le Quotidien., 2020a. "Foncier Lotissement De 62 Ha Entre L'aéroport De Dakar, La Boa … : Ngor Scandalisé," Le Quotidien.sn, June 23. www.lequotidien.sn/foncier-lotissement-de-62-ha-entre-laeroport-de-dakar-la-boa-ngor-scandalise/ (Accessed May 3, 2024).

Le Quotidien., 2020b. "Après avoir reçu un mouvement de revendication: Le ministre Oumar Youm «divise» les jeunes de Cambérène," LeQuotidien.sn, June 27. www.lequotidien.sn/apres-avoir-recu-un-mouvement-de-revendication-le-ministre-oumar-youm-divise-les-jeunes-de-camberene/ (Accessed May 3, 2024).

LeBas, A., 2020. Who trusts? Ethnicity, integration, and attitudes toward elected officials in urban Nigeria. *Comparative Political Studies*, 53(10–11), pp.1738–1766.

Leonard, D. K., 2008. *Where are "pockets" of effective agencies likely in weak governance states and why?: A propositional inventory*. Institute of Development Studies at the University of Sussex.

Leral.net., 2022. "Ouverture du pont de Cambérène: Les populations partagées," March 3. www.leral.net/Ouverture-du-pont-de-Camberene-Les-populations-partagees_a326143.html.

Levenson, Z., 2018. The road to TRAs is paved with good intentions: Dispossession through delivery in post-apartheid Cape Town. *Urban Studies*, 55(14), pp.3218–3233.

Levi, M. and Stoker, L., 2000. Political trust and trustworthiness. *Annual Review of Political Science*, *3*(1), pp.475–507.

Lewis, P. and Stein, H., 1997. Shifting fortunes: The political economy of financial liberalization in Nigeria. *World Development*, *25*(1), pp.5–22.

Limao, N. and Venables, A. J., 2001. Infrastructure, geographical disadvantage, transport costs, and trade. *The World Bank Economic Review*, *15*(3), pp.451–479.

Lipton, M., 2023. Why poor people stay poor. In Harriss, J. ed. *Rural development: Theories of peasant economy and agrarian change* (pp.66–81). Routledge.

Magassouba, M., 1985. *L'Islam au Senegal: Demain les Mollahs?* Karthala.

Mahoney, J., 2004. Comparative-historical methodology. *Annual Review of Sociology*, *30*(1), pp.81–101.

Mamdani, M., 1996. *Citizen and subject: Africa and the legacy of late colonialism*. Princeton University Press.

Mamdani, M., 2002. *When victims become killers: Colonialism, nativism, and the genocide in Rwanda*. Princeton University Press.

Maney, G. M. and Abraham, M., 2008. Whose backyard? Boundary making in NIMBY opposition to immigrant services. *Social Justice*, *35*(4), pp.66–82.

Mann, M., 1984. The autonomous power of the state: Its origins, mechanisms and results. *European Journal of Sociology/Archives européennes de sociologie*, *25*(2), pp.185–213.

Mann, M., 2005. *The dark side of democracy: Explaining ethnic cleansing*. Cambridge University Press.

Mann, M., 2008. Infrastructural power revisited. *Studies in Comparative International Development*, *43*, pp.355–365.

Mazrui, A. A., 1995. The blood of experience: The failed state and political collapse in Africa. *World Policy Journal*, *12*(1), pp.28–34.

Mbacké, K., 2005. *Sufism and religious brotherhoods in Senegal*. Markus Wiener.

Mbacké, M. M., Ndao, M. L., and Ndonky, A., 2024. Urban dynamics and emergence of new centers in the Dakar region (Senegal). *Journal of Geographic Information System*, *16*(4), pp.227–243.

Mbembe, A., 2001. *On the postcolony* (Vol. 41). University of California Press.

M'bokolo, E., 1982. Peste et société urbaine à Dakar: l'épidémie de 1914. *Cahiers d'études africaines*, 22(85/86), pp.13–46.

McAvoy, G. E., 1998. Partisan probing and democratic decisionmaking rethinking the Nimby syndrome. *Policy Studies Journal*, *26*(2), pp.274–292.

McClintock, N., 2015. A critical physical geography of urban soil contamination. *Geoforum*, *65*, pp.69–85.

McFarlane, C. and Rutherford, J., 2008. Political infrastructures: Governing and experiencing the fabric of the city. *International Journal of Urban and Regional Research*, *32*(2), pp.363–374.

McNee, G. and Pojani, D., 2022. NIMBYism as a barrier to housing and social mix in San Francisco. *Journal of Housing and the Built Environment*, *37*(1), pp.553–573.

Mercier, P. and Balandier, G., 1953. *Les pêcheurs Lébou du Sénégal*. Centre IFAN-Sénégal.

Migdal, J. S., 1988. *Strong societies and weak states: State-society relations and state capabilities in the third world*. Princeton University Press.

Mkandawire, P. T. and Soludo, C. C., 1999. *Our continent, our future: African perspectives on structural adjustment*. Idrc.

Mkandawire, T., 2001. Thinking about developmental states in Africa. *Cambridge Journal of Economics*, *25*(3), pp.289–314.

Mohl, R. A., 2014. Citizen activism and freeway revolts in Memphis and Nashville: The road to litigation. *Journal of Urban History*, *40*(5), pp.870–893.

Moore, M. and Schneider, A., 2004. *Taxation, governance and poverty: Where do the middle income countries fit?* Institute of Development Studies.

Müller-Crepon, C., Hunziker, P., and Cederman, L. E., 2021. Roads to rule, roads to rebel: Relational state capacity and conflict in Africa. *Journal of Conflict Resolution*, *65*(2–3), pp.563–590.

Murphy, W. P. and Bledsoe, C. H., 1987. Kinship and territory in the history of a Kpelle chiefdom (Liberia). In Kopytoff, I. ed. *The African frontier: The reproduction of traditional African societies* (pp.123–147). Indiana University Press.

Naím, M., 1994. Latin America: The second stage of reform. *Journal of Democracy*, *5*, p.32.

Ndegwa, S. and Levy, B., 2003. *The politics of decentralization in Africa: A comparative analysis*. The World Bank.

Ndiaye. A., 2018. "Prolongement de la VDN à Cambérène: les populations menacent de bloquer les travaux dans 48 heures," Pressafrik, April 5. www.pressafrik.com/%E2%80%8BProlongement-de-la-VDN-a-Camberene-les-populations-menacent-de-bloquer-les-travaux-dans-48-heures_a180874.html (Accessed May 3, 2024).

N'diaye, A. H., 2008. *Le rôle des confréries musulmanes dans les institutions et la vie politique et sociale du Sénégal* (Doctoral dissertation, Paris 2).

Ndiaye, F. 2018a. "Sénégal: Destruction du mur construit sur l'emprise du prolongement de la VDN – L'etat recule, face à la pression de Cambérène," Sud Quotidien, July 4. https://fr.allafrica.com/stories/201807050339.html (Accessed May 3, 2024).

Ndiaye, F., 2018b. "Sénégal: Livraison de la seconde partie de la VDN en fin d'année – L'etat s'engage à respecter les délais," Sud Quotidien. July 4. https://fr.allafrica.com/stories/201807050378.html (Accessed May 6, 2024).

Ndiaye, I., 2015. Étalement urbain et différenciation sociospatiale à Dakar (Sénégal). *Cahiers de géographie du Québec*, *59*(166), pp.47–69.

Ndiaye, M., 2021. Au coeur de la gouvernance locale: Parcelles Assainies: une commune, 4 problématiques majeures. L'Harmattan.

Ndiaye, S., 2019. "Absence de Passerelles: Des Accidents Fréquents sur le Prolongement de la VDN," *Senegal7.com*, July 23. https://senegal7.com/absence-de-passerelles-des-accidents-frequents-sur-le-prolongement-de-la-vdn/ (Accessed May 6, 2024).

Ndiaye, T., 2020a. "Spoliation foncière dans le cadre du projet 'Une famille, un toit': Dougar réclame ses terres," Seneweb.com, August 13. www.seneweb.com/news/Societe/spoliation-fonciere-dans-le-cadre-du-pro_n_326171.html. (Accessed May 3, 2024).

Ndiaye, T., 2020b. "[Photos] Expulsions à Terme Sud: Ça chauffe entre les éléments de la Dscos et les 79 familles militaires," Seneweb.com, September 30. www.seneweb.com/news/Video/ouakam-expulsions-a-terme-sud-ca-chauffe_n_329948.html (Accessed May 3, 2024).

Ndiaye, T., 2024a. [Prolongement de la Vdn, 10 ans après] Changement de tracé, route accidentogène, accès risqué à la mer: Danger sur la Voie de Dégradation du littoral Nord ! [1/4]. » Seneweb.com, October 9. www.seneweb.com/news/Dossier%20de%20la%20redaction/changement-de-trace-route-accidentogene-_n_452724.html. (Accessed October 29, 2024)

Ndiaye, T. 2024b. "[Prolongement de la Vdn, 10 ans après] Déclassement de la bande de filaos: À qui profite le crime? (4/4)," Seneweb.com, October 23. www.seneweb.com/news/Dossier%20de%20la%20redaction/declassement-de-la-bande-de-filaos-a-qui_n_453949.html (Accessed October 28, 2024).

Ndiaye, T. M., 2020. "Camberène: La guerre des mouvements de jeunes sur les travaux de la VDN," Senego.com, June 26. https://senego.com/camberene-la-guerre-des-mouvements-de-jeunes-sur-les-travaux-de-la-vdn_1113148.html. (Accessed May 3, 2024).

Ndlovu-Gatsheni, S. J., 2013. *Coloniality of power in postcolonial Africa*. African Books Collective.

Ndulu, B. J., 2006. Infrastructure, regional integration and growth in sub-Saharan Africa: Dealing with the disadvantages of geography and sovereign fragmentation. *Journal of African Economies*, *15*(suppl_2), pp.212–244.

Nega, B. and Schneider, G., 2014. NGOs, the state, and development in Africa. *Review of Social Economy*, *72*(4), pp.485–503.

Nettali.com, 2019. "VDN 2 de Cambérène: Les Malentendus Levés, les Travaux Redémarrent," *Nettali.com*, September 18. www.nettali.com/2019/09/18/vdn-2-de-camberene-les-malentendus-leves-les-travaux-redemarrent/ (Accessed May 3, 2024).

Niakaar., 2020. "Scandale Foncier À Ouakam: De Gros Pontes Du Pouvoir Encore Mouillés!," Xibaaru.sn. May 13. www.xibaaru.sn/scandale-foncier-a-ouakam-de-gros-pontes-du-pouvoir-encore-mouilles/ (Accessed May 3, 2024).

Njoh, A. J., 2000. Transportation infrastructure and economic development in sub-Saharan Africa. *Public Works Management & Policy*, 4(4), pp.286–296.

Njoh, A. J., 2009. Urban planning as a tool of power and social control in colonial Africa. *Planning Perspectives*, 24(3), pp.301–317.

Njoh, A. J., 2013. Equity, fairness and justice implications of land tenure formalization in C ameroon. *International Journal of Urban and Regional Research*, 37(2), pp.750–768.

Njoh, A. J., 2017. "The right-to-the-city question" and indigenous urban populations in capital cities in Cameroon. *Journal of Asian and African Studies*, 52(2), pp.188–200.

Nugent, P., 2018. Africa's re-enchantment with big infrastructure: White elephants dancing in virtuous circles? In Schubert, J., Engel, U., and Macamo, E. eds. *Extractive industries and changing state dynamics in Africa* (pp.22–40). Routledge.

Nyamnjoh, B., 2016. *#RhodesMustFall: Nibbling at resilient colonialism in South Africa*. African Books Collective.

Obadare, E., 2005. A crisis of trust: History, politics, religion and the polio controversy in Northern Nigeria. *Patterns of Prejudice*, 39(3), pp.265–284.

Obadare, E., 2009. The uses of ridicule: Humour,"infrapolitics" and civil society in Nigeria. *African Affairs*, 108(431), pp.241–261.

Obeng-Odoom, F., 2013. The state of African cities 2010: Governance, inequality and urban land markets. *Cities*, 31, pp.425–429.

O'brien, R. C., 1972. *White society in black Africa: The French of Senegal*. Faber & Faber.

Okeyinka, Y., 2014. Housing in the third world cities and sustainable urban developments. *Developing Country Studies*, 4(8), pp.112–120.

Olson Jr, M., 1971. *The logic of collective action: Public goods and the theory of groups, with a new preface and appendix* (Vol. 124). Harvard University Press.

Olukoshi, A. O., 1998. *The elusive Prince of Denmark: Structural adjustment and the crisis of governance in Africa* (No. 104). Nordic Africa Institute.

Ombati, M., 2017. "Gifts of Art for Kenyan (M) Pigs": Festival of resistance against elite impunity in Kenya. *Africa Development*, 42(2), pp.193–216.

Onoma, A. K., 2009. *The politics of property rights institutions in Africa*. Cambridge University Press.

Onoma, A. K., 2013. *Anti-refugee violence and African politics*. Cambridge University Press.

Onoma, A. K., 2018. Epidemics and intra-communal contestations: Ekeh,"les Guinéens" and Ebola in West Africa. *The Journal of Modern African Studies*, 56(4), pp.595–617.

Onoma, A. K., 2020. Xenophobia's contours during an Ebola epidemic: Proximity and the targeting of Peul migrants in Senegal. *African Studies Review*, 63(2), pp.353–374.

ONU Habitat, 2012. *"Profil du Secteur du Logement au Senegal."* Programme des Nations unies pour les etablissements humains.

Osaghae, E. E., 1995. Amoral politics and democratic instability in Africa: A theoretical exploration. *Nordic Journal of African Studies*, 4(1), pp. 62–78.

Osaghae, E. E., 1997. The role of civil society in consolidating democracy-an African comparative perspective. *Africa Insight*, 27(1), pp.15–23.

Osseo-Asare, A. D., 2016. "Atomic lands": Understanding land disputes near Ghana's nuclear reactor. *African Affairs*, 115(460), pp.443–465.

Owuor, S. and Mbatia, T., 2012. Nairobi. In Bekker, S.B. and Therborn, G., eds. *Capital cities in Africa: Power and powerlessness* (pp.120–141). HSRC Press.

Owusu, F., 2006. On public organizations in Ghana: What differentiates good performers from poor performers? *African Development Review*, 18(3), pp.471–485.

Paller, J. W., 2015. Informal networks and access to power to obtain housing in urban slums in Ghana. *Africa Today*, 62(1), pp.31–55.

Paller, J. W., 2019. *Democracy in Ghana: Everyday politics in urban Africa*. Cambridge University Press.

Parsons, T., 1997. "Kibra is our blood": The Sudanese military legacy in Nairobi's Kibera location, 1902–1968. *The International Journal of African Historical Studies*, 30(1), pp.87–122.

Pasotti, E., 2020. *Resisting redevelopment: Protest in aspiring global cities*. Cambridge University Press.

Pierson, P., 2000. Not just what, but when: Timing and sequence in political processes. *Studies in American Political Development*, 14(1), pp.72–92.

Polanyi, K., 2001. *The great transformation: The political and economic origins of our time*. Beacon press.

Pons, V., 1969. *Stanleyville: An African Urban Community under Belgian Administration*. Oxford University Press.

Prichard, W. and Leonard, D. K., 2010. Does reliance on tax revenue build state capacity in sub-Saharan Africa? *International Review of Administrative Sciences*, *76*(4), pp.653–675.

Purdeková, A., 2011. "Even if I am not here, there are so many eyes": Surveillance and state reach in Rwanda. *The Journal of Modern African Studies*, *49*(3), pp.475–497.

Putnam, R. D., 1994. Making democracy work: Civic traditions in modern Italy. Princeton University Press.

Putnam, R. D., 1995. Tuning in, tuning out: The strange disappearance of social capital in America. *PS: Political Science & Politics*, *28*(4), pp.664–683.

Rakodi, C., 1997. Global forces, urban change, and urban management in Africa. In Rakodi, C. ed. *The urban challenge in Africa: Growth and management of its large cities* (pp.17–73). Brookings Institution Press.

Ranganathan, M., 2014. Paying for pipes, claiming citizenship: Political agency and water reforms at the urban periphery. *International Journal of Urban and Regional Research*, *38*(2), pp.590–608.

Rassoul, E., 2019. "Le Viaduc de la VDN 2 Ouvert sur Camberene," February 4. www.au-senegal.com/le-viaduc-de-la-vdn-2-ouverte-sur-camberene,15603.html?lang=fr.

Rathbone, R., 2000. *Nkrumah & the chiefs: The politics of chieftaincy in Ghana, 1951–60*. Ohio State University Press.

Rayfield, J. R., 1974. Theories of urbanization and the colonial city in West Africa. *Africa*, *44*(2), pp.163–185.

Ren, X. and Weinstein, L., 2013. Urban governance, mega-projects and scalar transformations in China and India. In Samara, T., He, S., and Chen, G., eds. *Locating right to the city in the global south* (pp.107–126). Routledge.

Reno, W., 1998. *Warlord politics and African states*. Lynne Rienner.

Resnick, D. and Sivasubramanian, B., 2023. Political trust and informal traders in African cities. *The Journal of Modern African Studies*, *61*(3), pp.389–412.

Rimondi, L., 2015. RDC: Filimbi, la nouvelle génération de citoyens qui ébranle le pouvoir. *Éclairage du GRIP*, August 17, pp.1–4.

Riviere, C., 1971. *Mutations Sociales en Guinée*. Editions Marcel Riviere et Cie.

Ross, E., 2013. Christmas in Cambérène, or how Muhammad begets Jesus in Senegal. In Cormack, M. ed. *Muslims and others in sacred space* (pp.74–107). Oxford University Press.

Rothchild, D., 1991. Ghana and structural adjustment: An overview. In Rothchild, D. ed. *Ghana: The political economy of recovery* (pp.3–17). Lynne Rienner.

Sall, T. A., 2020. "Depredation Fonciere Et Engagement Politique," SenePlus, August 22. www.seneplus.com/opinions/depredation-fonciere-et-engagement-politique (Accessed May 3, 2024).

Samatar, A. I., 1999. An African miracle: State and class leadership, and colonial legacy in Botswana development. Heinemann.

Sandberg, S., 2010. What can "lies" tell us about life? Notes towards a framework of narrative criminology. *Journal of Criminal Justice Education*, *21*(4), pp.447–465.

Sané, Y., 2013. La politique de l'habitat au Sénégal: une mutation permanente? *Les Cahiers d'Outre-Mer*, *263*, pp.311–334.

Sarr, Y., 1984. Up from scratch: The sites and services approach to housing in Senegal. *IDRC reports, v. 12, no. 4, pp. 8-10*.

Schatz, E., 2009. Introduction: Ethnographic immersion and the study of politics. In Schatz, E. ed. *Political ethnography: What immersion contributes to the study of power* (pp. 13–34). University of Chicago Press.

Schively, C., 2007. Understanding the NIMBY and LULU phenomena: Reassessing our knowledge base and informing future research. *Journal of Planning Literature*, *21*(3), pp.255–266.

Schneider, B. R., 1991. *Politics within the state: Elite bureaucrats and industrial policy in authoritarian Brazil*. University of Pittsburgh Pre.

Schneider, B. R., 1998. Elusive synergy: Business-government relations and development. *Comparative Politics*, *31*(1), pp.101–122.

Scott, J. C., 1999. *Seeing like a state: How certain schemes to improve the human condition have failed*. Yale University Press.

Scott, J. C., 1990. *Domination and the arts of resistance: Hidden transcripts*. Yale University Press.

Scott, J. C., 2009. *The art of not being governed: An anarchist history of upland Southeast Asia*. Yale University Press.

Scott, J. C., 2012. *Two cheers for anarchism: Six easy pieces on autonomy, dignity, and meaningful work and play*. Princeton University Press.

Seay, L., 2010. Post-conflict authority and state reconstruction in the eastern democratic republic of the Congo. In Falola, T. and Njoku, R. eds. *War and Peace in Africa: History, Nationalism, and the State* (pp. 517–534). Carolina Academic Press.

Seck, A., 1968. Dakar, ville champignon. In Sankale, M., Thomas, L. V., and Fougeyrollas, P. eds. *Dakar en Devenir* (pp.17–47). Presence Africaine.

Seck, A., 1970. "Dakar: Metropole Ouest-Africaine" (Master's Thesis, Institute Fondamental d'Afrique Noire).

Sellers, J. M., 2019. From within to between nations: Subnational comparison across borders. *Perspectives on Politics*, *17*(1), pp.85–105.

Sender, J. and Smith, S., 1985. What's right with the Berg report and what's left of its critics? *Capital & Class*, *8*(3), pp.125–146.

Seneweb News, 2019. "VDN 3: 12 Personnes Tuées en 6 Mois," *Seneweb.com*, August 5. www.seneweb.com/news/Societe/vdn-3-12-personnes-tuees-en-6-mois_n_290252.html (Accessed May 6, 2024).

Seye, B., 2022. "Foncier – Ngor, Ouakam, Yoff, Rufisque, Bargny: Des investisseurs servis au détriment des populations," Enquete+, March 2. www.enqueteplus.com/content/foncier-ngor-ouakam-yoff-rufis que-bargny-des-investisseurs-servis-au-détriment-des (Accessed May 3, 2024).

Sidibé, I., 2013. Un territoire littoral dans l'espace politique, économique et religieux du Sénégal. Le cas de la baie de Ouakam (Dakar). *Espace populations sociétés: Space Populations Societies*, (1–2), pp.159–176.

Sidibé, I., 2015. Enquête dans des quartiers traditionnels du littoral dakarois, Sénégal: quelle action publique? *Géocarrefour*, *90*(90/1), pp.73–82.

Sietchiping, R., Permezel, M. J., and Ngomsi, C., 2012. Transport and mobility in sub-Saharan African cities: An overview of practices, lessons and options for improvements. *Cities*, *29*(3), pp.183–189.

Simone, A., 2010. *City life from Jakarta to Dakar: Movements at the crossroads*. Routledge.

Simone, A. M., 2004. *For the city yet to come: Changing African life in four cities*. Duke University Press.

Singh, A., 2020. The myth of "debt-trap diplomacy" and realities of Chinese development finance. *Third World Quarterly*, *42*(2), pp.239–253.

Snary, C., 2004. Understanding risk: The planning officers' perspective. *Urban Studies*, *41*(1), pp.33–55.

Snyder, R., 2001. Scaling down: The subnational comparative method. *Studies in Comparative International Development*, *36*, pp.93–110.

Southall, A., 1989. The African port city: Docks and suburbs. *Economic Development and Cultural Change*, *38*(1), pp.167–189,

Sow, A., 2019. "PA, U15: Les Riverains Barrent la VDN Pour Réclamer des Passerelles de Protection," sanslimitesn.com, July 20. https://sanslimitesn.com/pa-u15-les-riverains-barrent-la-vdn-pour-reclamer-des-passerelles-de-protection/ (Accessed May 6, 2024).

Sow, C. O., 2013. "'Pourquoi Nos Gouvernants Ne Veulent Pas De La Reforme Fonciere De Me Doudou Ndoye': Aliou Diack, Ancien President De La Communaute Rurale De Mbane," Seneplus, December 19. www.seneplus.com/article/pourquoi-nos-gouvernants-ne-veulent-pas-de-la-reforme-fon ciere-de-me-doudou-ndoye (Accessed May 3, 2024).

Sow, F., 1983. Pikine, Senegal: A reading of a contemporary African city. In Taylor, B., ed. *Reading the Contemporary African City* (pp. 45–60). Concept Media Pte Ltd.

Splinter, E. and Van Leynseele, Y., 2019. The conditional city: Emerging properties of Kenya's satellite cities. *International Planning Studies*, *24*(3–4), pp.308–324.

Strauss, J. C., 1998. *Strong institutions in weak polities: State building in Republican China, 1927–1940*. Oxford University Press.

Suret-Canale, J., 1971. *French colonialism in tropical Africa, 1900–1945*. Pica Press.

Sy, J. H., Diallo, M. A. et Kane, P. S., 2009. "*Le domaine public maritime de Dakar: élites, pouvoir et impunité,*" Rapport de l'ONG Aide Transparence.

Sylla, A., 1955. Une République Africane au XIX e siècle (1795–1857). *Présence africaine*, 1/2 (April–July), pp.47–65.

Sylla, A., 1971. Les persecutions de Seydina Mouhamadou Limamou Lâye par les autorités coloniales. *Bulletin de l'Institut Fondamental d'Afrique Noire, Série B: Sciences humaines*, *33*(3), pp.590–641.

Sylla, A., 1992. *Le peuple Lebou de la presqu'île du Cap-Vert*. Les nouvelles éditions africaines du Sénégal.

Taiwo, O., 2010. *How colonialism preempted modernity in Africa*. Indiana University Press.

Tall, M. S., 1994. Les investissements immobiliers à Dakar des émigrants sénégalais. *Revue européenne des migrations internationales*, *10*(3), pp.137–151.

Tati, G., 2012. Brazzaville. *Capital cities in Africa: Power and powerlessness*. pp.104–119.

Thelen, K., 2004. *How institutions evolve: The political economy of skills in Germany, Britain, the United States, and Japan*. Cambridge University Press.

Thelen, K. and Mahoney, J., 2015. Comparative-historical analysis in contemporary political science. *Advances in Comparative Historical Analysis*, *3*, p.36.

Thiam, M., 2019. "Sénégal: Insécurité routière – 13% des accidents mortels touchent les jeunes de moins de 18 ans," Sud Quotidien. https://fr.allafrica.com/stories/201905110156.html (Accessed May 6, 2024).

Tilly, C., 1985. Models and realities of popular collective action. *Social Research*, pp.717–747.

Touré, O. and Seck, M. S., 2013. "Amelioration de la gouvernance fonciere au Senegal: enjeux actuels et les defis pour l'avenir," GRET Fiche Pays no. 3: Senegal (November).

References

Tuori, K., 2015. The theory and practice of indigenous dispossession in the late nineteenth century: The Saami in the far north of Europe and the legal history of colonialism. *Comparative Legal History*, 3(1), pp.152–185.

Ukiwo, U., 2005. The study of ethnicity in Nigeria. *Oxford Development Studies*, 33(1), pp.7–23.

Van Arkadie, B., 1995. *The state and economic change in Africa* (pp.31–50). Oxford: Clarendon Press.

Van de Walle, N., 2001. *African economies and the politics of permanent crisis, 1979–1999*. Cambridge University Press.

Van Gyampo, R. E. and Anyidoho, N. A., 2019. Youth politics in Africa. In *Oxford Research Encyclopedia: Politics*, edited by W. R. Thompson. Oxford University Press. Accessed April 18, p.2022.

Vernière, M., 1973. Pikine, "ville nouvelle" de Dakar, un cas de pseudo-urbanisation. *L'Espace géographique*, 2(2), pp.107–126.

Vernière, M., 1977. *Dakar et son double Dagoudane Pikine*. Imprimerie nationale.

Villalón, L. A., 1995. *Islamic society and state power in Senegal: Disciples and citizens in Fatick*. Cambridge University Press.

Wakely, P., 2018. *Housing in developing cities: Experience and lessons*. Routledge.

Wang, Y., Shen, C., Bartsch, K., and Zuo, J., 2021. Exploring the trade-off between benefit and risk perception of NIMBY facility: A social cognitive theory model. *Environmental Impact Assessment Review*, 87, p.106555.

Wedeen, L., 2010. Reflections on ethnographic work in political science. *Annual Review of Political Science*, 13, pp.255–272.

Weinstein, L., 2013. Demolition and dispossession: Toward an understanding of state violence in millennial Mumbai. *Studies in Comparative International Development*, 48, pp.285–307.

Weinstein, L. and Ren, X. (2009). The changing right to the city: Urban renewal and housing rights in globalizing Shanghai and Mumbai. *City & Community*, 8(4), pp.407–432. https://doi.org/10.1111/j.1540-6040.2009.01300.x.

White, R. R., 1985. The impact of policy conflict on the implementation of a government-assisted housing project in Senegal. *Canadian Journal of African Studies/La Revue canadienne des études africaines*, 19(3), pp.505–528.

Willems, W., 2019. "The politics of things": Digital media, urban space, and the materiality of publics. *Media, Culture & Society*, 41(8), pp.1192–1209.

Wolsink, M., 2000. Wind power and the NIMBY-myth: Institutional capacity and the limited significance of public support. *Renewable Energy*, 21(1), pp.49–64.

World Bank, 1981. *Accelerated development in sub-Saharan Africa: An agenda for action*. World Bank Group.

World Bank, 1997. The state in a changing world. *World Development Report*. World Bank Group.

World Bank, 2002. Building institutions for markets. *World Development Report*. The World Bank.

World Bank, 2015. "Revue de l'urbanisation: Villes emergentes pour un Senegal emergeant," GSURR Africa Revue no. ACS14161.

Wright, G., 1991. *The politics of design in French colonial urbanism*. University of Chicago Press.

Xalimasn, 2018., "Destruction du mur de Camberene: Face a la pression des Layenes, Macky Recule," Xalima.com, July 4. https://xalimasn.com/destruction-du-mur-de-camberene-face-a-la-pression-des-layenes-macky-recule/ (Accessed May 3, 2024).

Young, C., 2018. Africa: An interim balance sheet. In Lewis, P. ed. *Africa: Dilemmas of development and change*(pp.341–358). Routledge.

Zeleza, P. T., 1993. *A modern economic history of Africa: The nineteenth century* (Vol. 1). CODESRIA.

Acknowledgments

I wish to thank Mamadou Fallou Diouf, Serigne Diop, and Cheikh Ka for research assistance for this work. I also wish to thank Jeff Paller, Rachel Riedl, Maya Tudor, Ben Ross Schneider, and two anonymous reviewers of Cambridge University Press for their comments on drafts of this manuscript. My appreciation also goes to my former colleagues at CODESRIA – Marie Ndiaye, Emiliane Faye, Mamay Jah, Mame Sokhna Thiare, Abdon Sofonnou, Ndeye Aissatou Ndiaye, Bouchra Sidi-Hida, Divine Fuh, and Ibrahim Oanda – whose insights during our many discussions of politics in Senegal and in Africa more generally helped me pursue this project. A generous one-year Faculty Research Fellowship at the Jackman Humanities Institute at the University of Toronto helped me work on the final stages of this project.

Cambridge Elements

Politics of Development

Rachel Beatty Riedl
Einaudi Center for International Studies and Cornell University

Rachel Beatty Riedl is the Director and John S. Knight Professor of the Einaudi Center for International Studies and Professor in the Government Department and School of Public Policy at Cornell University. Riedl is the author of the award-winning *Authoritarian Origins of Democratic Party Systems in Africa* (2014) and co-author of *From Pews to Politics: Religious Sermons and Political Participation in Africa* (with Gwyneth McClendon, 2019). She studies democracy and institutions, governance, authoritarian regime legacies, and religion and politics in Africa. She serves on the Editorial Committee of World Politics and the Editorial Board of African Affairs, Comparative Political Studies, Journal of Democracy, and Africa Spectrum. She is co-host of the podcast Ufahamu Africa.

Ben Ross Schneider
Massachusetts Institute of Technology

Ben Ross Schneider is Ford International Professor of Political Science at MIT and Director of the MIT-Brazil program. Prior to moving to MIT in 2008, he taught at Princeton University and Northwestern University. His books include *Business Politics and the State in 20th Century Latin America* (2004), *Hierarchical Capitalism in Latin America* (2013), *Designing Industrial Policy in Latin America: Business-Government Relations and the New Developmentalism* (2015), and *New Order and Progress: Democracy and Development in Brazil* (2016). He has also written on topics such as economic reform, democratization, education, labor markets, inequality, and business groups.

Maya Tudor
Oxford University

Maya Tudor is Professor of Politics and Public Policy, Blavatnik School of Government and Fellow, St. Hilda's College, at Oxford University. She researches democracy and nationalism in the developing world, with a focus on South Asia, and is the author of two books, Promise of Power and Varieties of Nationalism.

Advisory Board
Yuen Yuen Ang, *University of Michigan*
Catherine Boone, *London School of Economics*
Melani Cammett, *Harvard University* (former editor)
Stephan Haggard, *University of California, San Diego*
Prerna Singh, *Brown University*
Dan Slater, *University of Michigan*

About the Series
The Element series *Politics of Development* provides important contributions on both established and new topics on the politics and political economy of developing countries. A particular priority is to give increased visibility to a dynamic and growing body of social science research that examines the political and social determinants of economic development, as well as the effects of different development models on political and social outcomes.

Cambridge Elements

Politics of Development

Elements in the Series

Democracy and Population Health
James W. McGuire

Rethinking the Resource Curse
Benjamin Smith and David Waldner

Greed and Guns: Imperial Origins of the Developing World
Atul Kohli

Everyday Choices: The Role of Competing Authorities and Social Institutions in Politics and Development
Ellen M. Lust

Locked Out of Development: Insiders and Outsiders in Arab Capitalism
Steffen Hertog

Power and Conviction: The Political Economy of Missionary Work in Colonial-Era Africa
Frank-Borge Wietzke

Varieties of Nationalism: Communities, Narratives, Identities
Harris Mylonas and Maya Tudor

Criminal Politics and Botched Development in Contemporary Latin America
Andreas E. Feldmann and Juan Pablo Luna

A Chinese Bureaucracy for Innovation-Driven Development?
Alexandre De Podestá Gomes and Tobias ten Brink

Claim-Making in Comparative Perspective: Everyday Citizenship Practice and Its Consequences
Janice K. Gallagher, Gabrielle Kruks-Wisner, and Whitney K. Taylor

Shocks and Politics: Understanding Disaster Preparedness
Jennifer Bussell

The Undulating Capacity of the State: Autochthony and Infrastructure Development in African Cities
Ato Kwamena Onoma

A full series listing is available at: www.cambridge.org/EPOD